Lexington Christian Fellowship

Children's Bible Study

Contents

"Telling the Story"

Now these are the commandments, the statutes, and the judgements, which the Lord your God commanded to teach you, that ye might do them in the Land whither ye go to possess it: That thou mightest fear the Lord thy God, to keep all his statutes and his commandments, which I command the, **thou, and thy son, and thy son's son,** *all the days of thy life: and that thy days may be prolonged.*

Hear therefore, O Israel, and observe to do it; that it may be well with thee, and that ye may increase mightily, as the **Lord God of thy fathers** *hath promised thee, in the land that floweth with milk and honey. Hear, O Israel: The Lord our God is one Lord: And thou shalt love the Lord thy God with all thine heart, and with all thy soul, and with all thy might.*

And these words, which I command thee this day, shall be in thine heart: **And thou shalt teach them diligently unto thy children,** *and shalt talk of them when thou sittest in thine house, and when thou walkest by the way, and when thou liest down, and when thou risest up. And thou shalt bind them for a sign upon thine hand, and they shall be as frontlets between thine eyes. And thou shalt write them upon the posts of thy house, and on thy gates.*

Deuteronomy 6:1-9

Point # I- Who is to teach our children the Word of God?

Our success in life depends on our obedience to the Word of God.

The passing on of the love of God and keeping His word is through example and precept.

It is the place of parents to teach "the commandments of God" to their children.

Point # 2-When and Where are we to teach the Word?

"and shalt talk of them when thou sittest in thine house, and when thou walkest by the way, and when thou liest down, and when thou risest up. And thou shalt bind them for a sign upon thine hand, and they shall be as frontlets between thine eyes. And thou shalt write them upon the posts of thy house, and on thy gates."

☐When thou sittest in thine house, and when thou walkest by the way,
☐When thou liest down and when thou risest up
☐And thou shalt bind them for a sign upon thine hand, and they shall be as frontlets between thine eyes.

◻And thou shalt write them upon the posts of thy house, and on thy gates.

Point #3-How do we teach them the Word?

"And when thy son asketh thee in time to come, saying, What mean the testimonies, and the statutes, and the judgments, which the Lord our God hath commanded you? Then thou shalt say unto thy son, We were Pharaoh's bondmen in Egypt; and the Lord brought us jout of Egypt with a mighty hand: And the Lord shewed signs and wonders, great and sore, upon Egypt, upon Pharaoh, and upon all his household, before our eyes: And he brought us out from thence that he might bring us in, to give us the land which he sware unto our fathers. And the Lord commanded us to do all these statutes, to fear the Lord our God, for our good always, that he might preserve us alive, as it is at this day."
Deuteronomy 6:20-25

◻Look for natural windows of opportunity

• *"And when thy son asketh thee in time to come,"*

◻Look for what peaks the attention of your children.

• *"When your children shall ask their fathers in time to come, saying, What mean these stones? Then ye shall let your children know, saying, Israel came over this Jordan on dry land."* Joshua 4:21-22

◻Connect the teachings of God with God's historical purposes.

• *We were Pharaoh's bondmen in Egypt; and the Lord brought us jout of Egypt with a mighty hand: And the Lord shewed signs and wonders, great and sore, upon Egypt, upon Pharaoh, and upon all his household, before our eyes: And he brought us out from thence that he might bring us in, to give us the land which he sware unto our fathers.*

•Learn to create a sense of destiny and history with your children.

•Share your testimony and younger life. Understand how God was working in you during that time.

◻Always give application to what you teach!

• *"And the Lord commanded us to do all these statutes, to fear the Lord our God, for our good always, that he might preserve us alive, as it is at this day."*

Our training program

The bible speaks of three kinds of learning:
- **Knowledge**
- **Experience**
- **Wisdom**

Knowledge is the cognitive accumulation of facts.
Experience is interacting with the natural and spiritual coarse of events *course*
and experiencing the consequences, both good and bad of that interaction.
Wisdom is understanding the consequences and choosing the right actions.

It is important for us to make sure that our children are exposed to all three aspects of learning. The cognitive accumulation of facts includes both Biblical and natural studies. It is the duty of a parent to make sure that a child receives both.

Whether or not a parent is supposed to teach their children science (as opposed to hiring a teacher) is debatable. However, the fact that God has made the parents responsible to teach (not have them taught) the scriptures is undisputable.

It is the parents place to teach their children the Bible.

At the same time, it is the responsibility of the church to teach every member.

The goal then, is for the church to help parents teach their own children, supplementing that teaching with gifted teachers. The teaching ministry of the church must never supplant the call of the parent.

(It is also important for the parent to be involved with giving a child responsibility and growing in wisdom as well. This area is covered more in our child training instruction.)

Scope

We plan to cover the Bible from cover to cover.

Sequence

We plan to have three units which last two years each:
- Old Testament Books of Law and History
- Old Testament Books of Poetry and Prophets
- New Testament Books

Structure

Parents will read through the Bible with their children, telling the Story as they go. Teachers will supplement with background materials and overviews.

Materials

Parents will use our notes for working through the story line.

Teachers (and parents) Will use, "What the Bible is all about - Quick reference edition", published by Regal Books, for background and supplemental materials.

Unit One-Old Testament Law and History

In unit one, the Parents purpose is to establish the story line of the Old Testament History.

Practical Advice

The Parent should keep the following things in mind:

☐ **You must know the big picture yourself.**
☐ **Don't get so caught up in the details that you forget the panoramic view.**
☐ **Remember these ongoing themes:**
   • **God's Covenant (Promise)**
   • **The progressive revelation of God**
   • **Christ and the plan of Salvation**
   • **Learn to weave these themes into your teaching of the OT.**

What is the big picture?

In eternity, God devised a plan to create an object for His love. That object was a man that He could engage in living with and communicating with and developing mutual relationship with the goal to making that man part of his family through marriage.

From the outset, God knew that man would be difficult to win and that it would cost Him his own life and peace. Knowing this, He still chose to create Adam. Along with Eve, Adam rebelled and introduced sin and rebellion to mankind. In the coming years, God began a tapestry which revealed His Mercy (This is the loving kindness of God which is a result of Him choosing to commit Himself in love to an individual.), His general nature and Character, and His purpose in Christ (to gather all things back to Himself).

After Adam's rebellion, the world degenerated into envy, murder, strife and everything that God is not. So, with Noah, He started over.

Then, surprise! Man still tried to live a life apart from God and He had to disperse them at Babel.

A few years later, God came to one man who could trust him and made a promise. God was interested in showing Abraham just how faithful He could be. It was with Abraham that God made his most famous OT Covenant. That is, "That he would be the father of many nations and bless the whole world."

The story becomes one of God keeping His promise to Abraham. God gives him a miracle son, then grandchildren and then finally a nation.

That nation was raised in Egypt so they would know the oppression of being separated from God.

Next, through Moses, God delivered the nation from bondage so that He could bring them into a land He had prepared for them.

After all this preparation, God called Israel to enter Canaan under Joshua and establish His house and become His people.

They did well for a while, but they got so caught up in their own land, that they forgot God's promise and their need for them.

He sent Judges to deliver them, but once delivered from enemies, they fell right back into the same old self-reliance and pride.

Finally, the people wanted more than judges. They asked for an earthly King like all the rest of the nations around them and they got one. He turned out to be just as fleshly as the rest.

God, in His mercy, raised up another King that was after His own heart, David. However, this didn't last long either. After David's Son, Solomon, the Kingdom split. There were some good kings and some bad kings. It went on for a few hundred years, but it was a downward spiral.

Finally, God raised up Assyria to take the northern tribes captive and a couple hundred years later, Babylon took Judah captive.

The northern tribes never returned, but Judah did come back under Zerubbabal, Ezra and Nehemiah.

The temple was rebuilt and the walls were restored, but they never saw the nation restored as it had been before.

Through this history, we see God:

Keeping His Character, Keeping His Word, Revealing Himself and Preparing man to receive Christ.

God knew man would not make it when He created Himself. He spent 4,000 years proving to man that no matter how he tried to be good enough, he could not.

So, after the perfect man failed, when the wealth of a nation or the power of a Kingdom would not work, when a new beginning wouldn't fix things, when prophets were stoned and priests went bad, when the nation had been reduced to a shadow of what it had once been, when wealth, poverty, success, failure, happiness and sadness could not bring man to God...

Christ came.

As a parent, it is your job to bring your child into this story. Know what God has done and where you and your family fit into HIS-story.

Bring it to life for yourself and for your family.

We are planning to cover the OT History in two years. You will find the reading guide in our text, "What the Bible is all about."

Here is what you need to do to get started:

1. **Go buy the book.**
2. **Get the notes.**
3. **Start reading the Bible, according to the guide, with your children.**
4. **Follow the notes each day to tell the story more fully.**
5. **Use Supper or bedtime to "tell the story" and bring your child into it.**

Sample:

Here is a sample of the first assignment

Week 1: Creation

Day 1
In the Beginning...God

Purpose of today's lesson: To explain that God has always been there and all that we see begins with Him.

Read Gen. 1

Ask where God came from.

Explain that God The Father, Jesus, and the Holy spirit worked together in creation. See John 1:1-3.

Here is what you do:
1. **Read the appropriate text yourself during the day.**
2. **Make sure the child reads it or is read to the night before.**
3. **At Supper, "Tell the Story"**

How to tell the Story

Purpose
Every Story has a purpose. Remember that the whole Bible is one story. Each little story is a chapter that builds toward the revelation of God and Christ. This should have bearing on how you tell the story.

Each smaller story may play several purposes in revealing God and His plan. As a parent, you must determine which purpose best trains your child. We have given suggested purposes which help build toward the greater themes.

Beginning
Every story must begin. How you begin the story is very important. Keeping your purpose in mind, your audience in mind and the story in mind, you must invite the audience into your story in a way that they will want to enter.

Remember the Biblical parents who responded to their children's curiosity about the pillar of rocks?

How could you start the story on this first day?

Maybe you could ask your child where he got a particular item (gameboy, shirt, book toy). Then you could ask how it got there (Gameboy at store). Then you could ask where

Store came from. Following this line, it won't be long before you get to God.

Then you say...That's right...God. All things come from God. Do you know where God came from? No! He didn't come from anywhere. He was always there.

Let me tell you something about God.

Next comes the Body of the story

There is only one God and He has always been there. But you know what? He is a family. He is a Father, Son and the Holy Spirit. They were all there and they were all part of the beginning. Just like we are one family but there are (#) of us, God is made up of three distinct members.

When they got ready to create the world and all that was in it, they had no disagreements, they all worked together to create the earth.

You know how we sometimes have trouble agreeing with how we want to do things? Well, God never disagrees with Himself.

So, when they got finished creating everything, you know what they said? God said, "this is very good."

The ending

Here is where you make your point.

"Do you worry about things? Did you know that the Bible says that we don't need to worry. We are God's children and He created everything. There is nothing bigger, better or smarter than Him."

He created you and the Bible says that you are in His image, that means like Him in a lot of ways. If you look with your heart you can see God's image in a lot of things.

You know how when we are just sitting on a log down by the creek or just being in nature. You know how it feels like your heart gets bigger and happiness fills your heart? That is because you are seeing God's image in nature.

We are in His image and that glorifies Him, nature carries His image and that glorifies Him all things glorify God one way or another.....Like this supper your mother made for us...Let's give thanks to God for Pizza.

Moral

Many of the stories will not address a moral in the body of the story. It is appropriate at the end to give a "moral" or "teaching" from the story.

Remember
- **Purpose**
- **Beginning**
- **Middle**
- **Ending**
- **Moral**

Assignment: Look at the other four days of week one and devise how you might "Tell the Story."

After the break, we will return and let different folks "Tell the Story."

Week 1: Creation

Day 1
In the Beginning...God

Purpose of todays lesson: To explain that God has always been there and all that we see begins wth Him.

Read Gen. 1

Ask where God came from.

Explain that God The Father, Jesus, and the Holy spirit worked together in creation. See John 1:1-3.

Day 2
Let there be...

Purpose of today's lesson: To explain how God created the world.

Ask what God used to make the world.

Explain that God spoke everything into existence by His Word. See Hebrews 1:3

Day 3
Let us create man in our own image...

Purpose: to discuss man in God's image.

Ask what image means.

Talk about how we are in God's image.

Day 4:
Have dominion

Purpose of todays lesson: To show God's purpose for man.

Ask what God intends for man to do. Why are we hear?

Show how God wants to use our lives to bring His Kingdom to the earth.

Day 5:
The beginning of marriage

Purpose: To discuss the goodness and purpose of marriage.

Ask why God said it was not good for man to be alone.

Explain the difference between Adam's role as a man and Eve's role as a woman.

Week 2: Fall

Day 1
The two trees

Purpose: To show that there are two ways of living life in relation to God [or, we can live in relationship with God or ourselves].

Ask: How are the two trees different?

Explain: One tree represents trusting self and the other tree represents trusting God.

Day 2
Doubting God

Purpose: To show that the root of all sin is doubting God.

Ask: What was the lie that Satan told?

Explain: We have all fallen for the big lie that God doesn't love us and we can't trust him.

Day 3
The result...

Purpose: God is holy and must punish sin.

Ask: Why did Adam and Eve hide from God?

Explain: Disobedience separates us from God.

Day 4
The cure...

Purpose: To show that there must be a sacrifice as atonement for sin.

Ask: Why did God make clothes of animal skins for Adam and Eve?

Explain: That the sacrifice of Jesus covers our sins.

Day 5
The promise

Purpose: To show that God prepared a way to restore man to Himself through Jesus.

Ask: Who is the seed of the woman?

Explain: God makes promises/covenants with .

Week 3: Flood

Day 1
Cain and Abel

Purpose: To show that God alone chooses what is acceptable to Him.

Ask: What is our acceptable worship to God?

Explain:

Day 2
Righteous Noah

Purpose: To show that God chooses people in every generation to carry out His purposes.

Ask: Why didn't God simply destroy everyone and start over?

Explain: That God is faithful to the covenants He makes.

Day 3
The Flood

Purpose: To show that God will ultimately judge sin.

Ask: What does the ark represent?

Explain: That the ark represents salvation in Jesus, and protection from God's judgement against sin.

Day 4

The Rainbow

Purpose: To demonstrate God's covenant mercy towards man

Ask: Why do you think God chose a rainbow as the sign of His covenant.

Explain: That God wanted a reminder that would be seen and known by all men.

Day 5
An Alter

Purpose: To show that God is pleased with sacrifice of His son.

Ask: Why did Noah kill the animals

Explain: That sacrifice of animals teaches us of the necessity of Jesus' sacrifice on behalf of man.

Week 4: Babel

Day 1
The Tower of Babel

Purpose: To show that none of man's achievments can bring Him into the presence of God.

Ask: Why didn't the people want to be scattered over the whole earth

Explain: That sinful man thinks of himself more highly than he ought.

Day 2
The Dispersion of Nations

Purpose: To show that separated from God humans are not able to maintain relationships.

Ask: Why are there so many countries in the world today.

Explain: That men, appart from God are never able to maintain peace and unity.

Day 3
Ham, Shem and Japeth

Purpose: To show that God desired to start fresh and fill the earth with His covenant people.

Ask: Why did God preserve Noah's children?

Explain: That God continued to carry out His covenant promise of salvation, and that he used Noah and His son's to extend His covenant reign over the earth.

Day 4
Abraham

Purpose: To teach that in the midst of judgement and human failure God coninues to prepare the way for the coming of His son.

Ask: Why did God tell Abraham to leave his country?

Explain: That God wanted to teach Abram to have a people reserved and set apart for Him.

Day 5
Review

Purpose: To review from creation to Abraham.

Ask: Ask the children to tell the Story of the first eleven chapters.

Explain: Be sure to follow the line of God's purpose, promise and His faithfulness to His word.

Week 5: Abraham

Day 1
Follow me

Purpose: To show that God calls us into personal relationship with Him.

Ask: Where was Abraham going?

Explain: That knowing what will happen in the future is not as important as obeying God now.

Day 2
The promise

Purpose: To show that God desires to use us to bless the world.

Ask: Why did God pick a man and woman who could no longer have children?

Explain: That God puts us in hopeless situations to teach us to hope in Him.

Day 3
Lot

Purpose: To show that love for the world is emnity with God.

Ask: Why did Lot have such a bad time of things?

Explain: That

Day 4
Ishmael

Purpose: To show that our abilities fall miserably short of carrying out God's plans.

Ask: Why did Abraham try Sarah's idea?

Explain: That we have many opportunities to fulfill God's call with our ideas, but we must do it God's way.

Week 6: Isaac

Day 1
Child of promise

Purpose: To show that God is faithful to His promises in His timing.

Ask: Why was Isaac called laughter?

Explain: That often God's promises seem impossible in our present circumstances.

Day 2
On the altar

Purpose: To show that God desires our hearts to be given to Him, and not to the blessings He gives us.

Ask: What is the significance of God's name in this story?

Explain: That when God requires something of us, he provides all that we need to meet that requirement.

Day 3

Finding a wife

Purpose: God teaches us what it means to be a servant.

Ask: What was the servants name?

Explain: That a true servant only takes pleasure when His master is blessed.

Day 4
The death of Abraham

Purpose: To teach us that God always keeps his promise, but in His own timing.

Ask: What happened to God's promise of making Abraham a great nation.

Explain: That God was continuing His covenant through Isaac.

Day 5
Two sons

Purpose: God sovreignly picks whomever He wishes to carry out His purposes.

Ask: Why didn't God pick the oldest son as the heir of the promise?

Explain: That God doesn't have to do things the way men do.

Week 7: Jacob

Day 1
Blessing and Birthright

Purpose: To show that God determines to work through us despite the flaws in our character.

Ask: Why did Jacob steal the birthright and the blessing?

Explain: That man tries to fulfill the destiny in his heart himself instead of waiting on God.

Day 2
Bethel

Purpose: To teach that God is faithful in making a way for us to come to Him.

Ask: Why do you use a ladder?

Explain Jesus is our ladder to God.

Day 3
Rachel, Leah, and Laban

Purpose: To show that God uses circumstances to teach us of our own character flaws.

Ask: How are Laban and Jacob alike?

Explain: That Laban did to Jacob what Jacob did to Esau.

Day 4
Peniel

Purpose: To show that each person must come face to face with God as they seek Him diligently.

Ask: Why did God give Jacob a limp to bless Him?

Explain: That God teaches us to know our weakness and need for Him.

Day 5
Jacob's name change

Purpose: To show that when we seek God with all our hearts we find Him.

Ask: What is the significance of Jacob's new name?

Explain: That God works in our character to make us like Him.

Week 8: Joseph

Day 1
The sons of Jacob

Purpose: To show that God is continuing to keep his promise to Abraham and is preparing for the nation of Israel.

Ask: How many brothers did Joseph have?

Explain: He had eleven brothers and they would become the twelve tribes of Israel.

Day 2
Joseph's dream and being sold

Purpose: To show that God has a destiny for his chosen.

Ask: Ask if they believe God has something special for them to do.

Explain: Explain that Joseph knew that he had something important to do, but that he didn't understand how it would happen.

Day 3
From success to jail

Purpose: To show that temptations come with success and that we must be faithful in that time.

Ask: If your child is ever tempted to do something wrong.

Explain: Sometimes people will turn on you just because you won't be a part of the bad thing they are doing. But you have a destiny and you can't waste it on foolish things.

Day 4
From jail to success

Purpose: To show that God always keeps his promise in His time.

Ask: Do you ever get tired of waiting? Waiting to get to do what an older brother does? Tired of waiting to have your own room? Tired of waiting to get to Grandma's house?

Explain: Sometimes, God is working things out so they are ready when we get there. When it is time, we will be where we need to be.

Day 5
Providing for Israel in the famine

Purpose: To show how God kept Joseph in order to bless all the tribes of Israel and that made Joseph part of God's promise keeping to Abraham.

Ask: Do you think God is going to use you in a special way? Why?

Explain: If God uses us in a special way, it is always to glorify His name and bring His purposes to pass.

Review of Genesis
Final week

Day 1
Four significant events

Purpose:
To review the first eleven chapters according to events

Ask: What are four major events in the first 11 chapters of the book?

Explain: From creation, to the fall, to the flood, to Babel, we see God working his purposes in the earth.

Day 2
Four Significant men.

Purpose:
To review the lives of the Patriarchs.

Ask: Who are the four significant men in Genesis beginning with Abraham

Explain: God began with Abraham and followed through to Joseph. Children should know Abraham, Isaac & Ishmael, Jacob and Esau, and the twelve sons of Jacob.

Day 3
Christ in the book of Genesis

Purpose:
To review where types or promises of Christ appeared in the book.

Ask: What do we hear about Christ in the Old Testament?

Explain: The promise to Adam and Eve, the ram in the thicket, the rainbow, etc.

Day 4
God's promise

Purpose: To show God's promises in the Book.

Ask: What are some of the promises God made in the book of Genesis.

Explain: The promise to Adam and Eve, The promise to Noah, the promise to Abraham.

Day 5
God's promise to us
Review pages 31-32 in the text.

Purpose: To show how we are partakers of God's promise to Abraham.

Explain: God began keeping his promise through Abraham, Isaac, Jacob and Joseph. Then share how Jesus was the completion of that promise and how we have been blessed through the promise to Abraham.

Exodus
Week 1

Day 1
Introduction

Page 33 in the text.

Day 2
The situation in Egypt

Purpose: To show what bondage to Sin will do to you.

Ask: What happened in 400 years to change the situation.

Explain: Joseph was dead and the new Pharaoh did not know the power of God. He wanted to use God's people for himself. Show the pain of serving sin.

Day 3
A deliverer is born

Purpose:
To show how God provides for His people.

Ask:
How was God going to deliver His people.

Explain: He was going to provide Moses as a deliverer. Show how God protected Moses and kept him safe in perilous times.

Day 4
Getting ahead of God

Purpose:
To show how getting ahead of God can get you in trouble.

Ask: Why did Moses have to leave Egypt
Ask: Do you ever get impatient or try to do things without God?

Explain: Moses was going to be used by God. However, he thought he could do it his way. God had a better idea.

EXODUS

Week 2: Oppression

Day 1
Multiplication (Ex 1:1-7)

Purpose of today's lesson: To show that God is continually faithful through history to his covenant promises.

Ask why the children of Israel multiplied.

Explain that God's purposes go far beyond our own generation.

Day 2
Seeds of Growth, the Blood of the Saints (Ex 1:8-14)

Purpose of today's lesson: To teach that God sometimes uses difficulty to advance His purpose.

Ask why the Israelites grew when oppressed.

Explain that God often uses suffering to cause us or His purposes to grow.

Day 3
A New Generation

Purpose of today's lesson: To explain that God must deal personally and experientially with all His children.

Ask why God allowed the Israelites to be oppressed.

Explain that God let's sin run its course so that we will know our need for him.

Day 4
Captive in Egypt (Ex 1:8-14)

Purpose of today's lesson: To show that we are helpless captives of sin.

Ask what Egypt represents to us today.

Explain that when we serve sin, we are its slaves.

Day 5
Destroying the Seed (Ex 1:15-22)

<u>Purpose of today's lesson</u>: **To show that Satan always attempts to abort the "seed" of the woman.**

Read Genesis 3:15

Ask what made Pharaoh try to kill the firstborn sons of Israel.

Explain that Satan always aggressively attacks the destiny that lies within the children of God.

Week 3: Called Out

Day 1
Called (Ex 2:1-10)

<u>Purpose of today's lesson</u>: **To show that God is sovereign, and draws each one of us from time and eternity to fellowship with Him in His purposes**

What is the significance of Moses' name?

Explain that God has chosen us and given each one of us a destiny long before we were born.

Day 2
Educated in Egypt (Acts 7:20-23)

<u>Purpose of today's lesson</u>: **To show that the best that man can do apart from God is a hindrance and a failure in God's eyes.**

Did God call Moses because of His wonderful education?

Explain that our giftings or talents are not important to God. He is interested in our character.

Day 3
Taking Matters into His Own Hands (Ex 2:11-14)

<u>Purpose of today's lesson</u>: To show that we cannot fulfill the longing for destiny in our hearts in the flesh or our own way.

Why did Moses kill the Egyptian?

Explain that having the call of God on your life does not necessarily mean that we have the character to carry it out.

Day 4
Back 40 (Ex 2:15-22)

<u>Purpose of today's lesson</u>: To show that God deals with us to teach us never to trust ourselves.

Was Moses wasting His time in the desert?

God is very patient to do what He needs to do to finish His work in us.

Day 5
Who's Plan? (Ex 2:23-25)

<u>Purpose of today's lesson</u>: To show that God desires to draw us into His plans and out of the misery of our own doing.

What made God listen to Israel's cry?

Explain that God always takes the initiative to draw us into His purposes. He wants relationship with us more that we want relationship with Him.

Week 4: The Burning Bush; Moses Returns

Day 1
Holy Ground in a Dry and Desolate Place (Ex 3:1-10)

<u>Purpose of today's lesson</u>: To show us that God is present in our times of desolation and testing and desires to speak to us during those times.

What was the state of Moses' heart when God spoke to him from the burning bush?

Explain that God came and renewed His call to Moses after his time in the desert.

Day 2

Purpose of today's lesson: To show that because of brokeness God's people are reluctant to respond to the call of God.

Why was Moses reluctant to accept the call of God?

Explain that Moses was completely broken by his prior experience and this lead him to believe that he was not worthy to be used by God.

Day 3
I Am (Ex 3:13-15)

Purpose of today's lesson: To show that God has all the resources to complete His plans on the Earth.

What is the meaning of God's name, "I AM"?

Explain how when God does a work in the earth God is the beginning and the end of that work and the people are vessels contributing nothing to the work.

Day 4
Signs for Moses (Ex 4:1-9)

Purpose of today's lesson: To show that God supports His vessel with specific gifts and powers for the mission at hand.

What were the two signs that Moses was to use when he presented himself to Israel?

Explain how God uses specific gifts and talents for the task at hand. God knew that Pharaoh would change his staff into snakes and thus see God's snake eat theirs. There was also special significance in the disease leprosy and the ability to bring it on and heal it.

Day 5
Aaron (Ex 4:10-17)

Purpose of today's lesson: To show that God's work is not based in one man but in an interdependent group of people.

Why did God call Aaron to help Moses?

Explain how God uses interdependent groups of people rather than "one man shows".

Week 5: Back in Egypt; Signs for Pharaoh

Day 1
Promise of Deliverance (Ex 4:18-31)

Purpose of today's lesson: To see that it is God's ultimate purpose to deliver His people from the bondage of sin and to expect resistance in pursuit of God's purpose.

Why did God tell Moses that Pharaoh would resist Moses and Israel would be delivered despite the resistance.

Explain that when God calls His people to a purpose there is often resistance and that God is faithful to come through despite the resistance.

Day 2
Ensuing Oppression (Ex 5)

Purpose of today's lesson: When we walk with God to overcome sin there is frequently severe oppression that comes against us.

What happened to the people of Israel when they asked to serve God?

Explain that tough times can follow those that choose to follow God.

Day 3
Signs for Pharaoh (Ex 6:1-7:9)

Purpose of today's lesson: When God delivers His people from sin, God completely crushes the power of sin as a sign to the sinner and the saint.

What did God tell Moses he was going to do to Pharaoh and to Egypt? Why?

Explain that it is not enough to bring God's people out from sin but the power of sin (Egypt) and the devil (Pharaoh) must be completely destroyed.

Day 4
The Ten Plagues (Ex 7:10-11:10)

Purpose of today's lesson: When the Lord destroys the power of an adversary (sin) the destruction is absolute, total and complete.

What were the ten plagues against Egypt and why were those plagues chosen?

Explain that each plague came directly against a god worshipped in Egypt and that God will destroy our own idols in the same way.

Day 5 (Ex 7:10-11:10)
Hard Heart

<u>Purpose of today's lesson</u>: **The deep roots of sin die hard.**

Why would Pharaoh continually refused to give in and harden his heart despite God's open demonstrations of power.

Explain that many times we foolishly hold on to the idols of our life even when God openly shows us what they are and how they have hurt us.

Week 6: Passover, Deliverance and Baptism

Day 1
The Lamb and its Blood (Ex 12:1-30)

<u>Purpose of today's lesson</u>: **God provides the sacrifice for sin whose blood causes the punishment for sin to passover those who trust in it.**

Describe how the Passover meal was to be prepared and how the blood was applied to each house.

Explain the relationship between Jesus and the Passover lamb and the role of the blood in preserving us from the penalty of sin.

Day 2
Deliverance (Ex 12:31-51, Ex 13:17-22)

<u>Purpose of today's lesson</u>: **As God had promised, the day came when His people are delivered from sin.**

What was it like when the people left Egypt?

Show that when God's people come out from sin that they are blessed and have what they need.

Day 3
Crossing the Red Sea (Ex 14:1-31)

<u>Purpose of today's lesson</u>: **God completed the deliverance in baptism.**

What is the relationship between Israel crossing the Red Sea and baptism of the believer?

Explain that even when the people came out of Egypt, Pharaoh came after them and was only completely defeated at the Red Sea. So sin will continue to pursue us and will come to ultimate defeat in baptism.

Day 4
Spontaneous Worship (Ex 15:1-21)

Purpose of today's lesson: When the believer meets with God the natural response is worship.

What did the people do on the other side of the Red Sea?

Show that worship is the natural response of the believer who has been with God.

Day 5
Consecrating the Firstborn (Ex 13:1-16)

Purpose of today's lesson: God uses special times, symbols and holidays to remind His people of His work in their lives.

Why did God have the Israelites consecrate their first born?

Explain that God wants us to remember His work in our lives and will use special times in our lives to remind us.

Week 7: The Wilderness

Day 1
Bitterness (Ex 15:22-27)

Purpose of today's lesson: To show us that the first thing in our hearts that needs to be dealt with is bitterness.

What was the first test of the Israelites in the wilderness and why?

Show that once we have come out of sin we have to deal with things in our own hearts that separate us from God like bitterness.

Day 2
What is it? (Ex 16:1-36)

<u>Purpose of today's lesson</u>: God provides for all the needs of His people in His own way.

What were the rules of the manna?

Explain that God desires to provide for His people but God does so in His own way and His own time.

Day 3
Water from the Rock (Ex 17:1-7; Jn 7:37-39)

<u>Purpose of today's lesson</u>: To show that the rock (Jesus) is the source for water (the Spirit) in the desert.

Why did God choose to give the people water from a rock?

Explain that the rock in the desert is Jesus who will give us the Holy Spirit when we come to Him.

Day 4
The First Battle (Ex 17:8-16)

<u>Purpose of today's lesson</u>: A people who are totally dependent on God can overcome its enemies.

Why did the army of the Israelites win when Moses' hands were up but lose when his hands were down?

Show that Moses' act was demonstrating complete surrender to God leading to victory and that we must be totally dependent in order to overcome our enemies in victory.

Day 5
Jethro (Ex 18:1-27)

<u>Purpose of today's lesson</u>: To show that authority and responsibility must be shared in the kingdom of God.

What was Jethro's advise to Moses and why?

Explain that it is God's plan to share but authority and responsibility in the kingdom.

Week 8: The Law

Day 1
Ten Commandments (Ex 19:1-20:26)

Purpose of today's lesson: To understand that the law was given to show the character of God and to bring us to Christ.

What were the ten commandments and why did God give them to Israel and to us?

Explain that the laws of God show us His character and make us come to God for help.

Day 2
"Laws of love" (Ex 22:1-23:13)

Purpose of today's lesson: To further understand the nature of the law and thus the nature of God as a God of love.

How do these laws add to what we have already learned from the ten commandments?

Explain how these laws further define the nature of God especially revealing God as a God of love.

Day 3
Hebrew Calendar (Ex 23:14-19)

Purpose of today's lesson: To see that God establishes holidays for the purpose of setting aside other things in life in order to focus on the Lord.

What were the three main Hebrew holidays and what was the meaning of each?

Explain that God creates special times for people to honor Him.

Day 4
God's Angel Prepares the Way (Ex 23:20-33)

Purpose of today's lesson: To show that God always goes before His people in order to establish them in His promises.

Why did the angel go into the land before the Israelites?

Explain how God does not send His people in alone to take the promise land but always sends His messengers in before them to establish them.

Day 5
Confirming the Covenant (Ex 24:1-18)

Purpose of today's lesson: God continually re-establishes His relationship with His people.

Why did Moses and the Hebrews perform the sacrifices again?

Explain how from time to time God has His people re-establish their commitment to Him so they will not forget their ultimate purpose.

Week 9: The Tabernacle

Day 1
The Meaning of "Tabernacle" (Ex 25:1-9)

Purpose of today's lesson: From the hearts of God's people come what is necessary to build the resting place of God.

How did God get what was needed to build a place where He would dwell?

Explain how gifts from the heart are necessary for the resting place of God.

Day 2
The Ark (Ex 25:10-22)

Purpose of today's lesson: God gives specific detailed instructions to His people in the construction of His dwelling place.

What were God's specific instructions on the construction of the ark?

Describe how the ark was constructed emphasizing the detail in building God's dwelling place.

Day 3
The Sacrifice (Ex 29:1-30:38)

Purpose of today's lesson: In the past God required complex offerings to be acceptable in His sight. Now we come to God by the complete sacrifice, Jesus Christ.

What were the offerings of the priests and why don't we have to do all these sacrifices?

Explain the offerings of the priests and how because of Jesus we don't have to do all those things.

Day 4
Priesthood (Ex 28:1-43, I Pet 2:9)

Purpose of today's lesson: **The priesthood, which we are a part of in Christ, had special garments that signified their relationship to God.**

What did the priests wear in their service to God?

Describe the garments of the priests emphasizing the ephod, the breastplate and the head piece.

Day 5
Sabbath (Ex 31:1-18, Isa 58:13,14)

Purpose of today's lesson: **God set apart the Sabbath as a reminder of our commitment to the Lord and our dependence on the Lord.**

What was the purpose of the Sabbath and how are we to observe it?

Explain the observation of the Sabbath and explain the purpose of the Sabbath.

Week 10: The Golden Calf and Completion of the Tabernacle

Day 1
Rebellion (Ex 32:1-14)

Purpose of today's lesson: **To show when people take their eyes off the one true God they will construct a false god to worship.**

What did the people do when they were separated from God?

Explain how when people are separated from God they will build a false god to worship.

Day 2
The Sword of Judgment (Ex 32:15-29)

Purpose of today's lesson: God cannot tolerate the worship of false gods.

What happens to people who worship false gods?

Explain that people who worship false gods suffer serious consequences.

Day 3
God's Offer to Moses (Ex 32:30-35)

Purpose of today's lesson: To show that God was committed to His man Moses and Moses was committed to the people of God.

What did Moses ask God to do and what did God promise to do?

Explain how Moses offered himself for the people and how God promised to go before Moses wherever he went.

Day 4
The Tent of Meeting (Ex 33:1-7)

Purpose of today's lesson: God put the place where people will meet with Him outside the gathering of the people.

Where did God move the place where people met with Him and why?

Explain how after the rebellion God moved His presence outside where the people were.

Day 5
The Glory of the Lord (Ex 33:18-23, Jn 1:18)

Purpose of today's lesson: No man can see the face of God and live yet we can see God through Jesus Christ.

What did God say when Moses asked to see His face?

Explain that in the Old Testament no man could look at God but through Jesus Christians can walk with God face to face.

Week 11: Review of Exodus

Day 1
The Call of Moses

Purpose of today's lesson: To review the call of the man of God and the life of a man used by God

Why did Moses do the things he did in the book of Exodus and how was he able to carry them out? How do you relate that to your life?

Explain that Moses was called by God to do what he did and what he accomplished was a result of Moses' dependence on God. We walk in the same manner as Moses.

Day 2
From Bondage to Freedom

Purpose of today's lesson: To show that God delivers people from bondage to freedom.

How were the people of Israel able to escape Egypt? What is something you need to be free from and how will you escape?

Explain that in every case Israel was able to escape from Egypt because of their trust in God and that as we trust in God we too will be able to escape our sin.

Day 3
The Wilderness

Purpose of today's lesson: To show that all of God's people go through times of testing in order to reveal problems and to get rid of them.

What were some of the trials that Israel endured in the wilderness and why did Israel have these problems?

Explain that sometimes trials come in the lives of God's people to show them their sinful ways and to help the people of God overcome their lack of faith.

Day 4
The Law

Purpose of today's lesson: To show that God's character is reflected in the Law and through the Law we can understand some of God's ways.

Why did God give us the Law?

Explain that the Law shows us who God is and brings us to Jesus.

Day 5
The Tabernacle of God

Purpose of today's lesson: To show that God will always have a place to meet with His people which is fashioned after His own design.

Where did God meet with the people of God then and where does He meet with us now?

Explain the place God met with Israel and where He meets with us today.

Leviticus

As we begin Leviticus it is a good time to look back and remember the "whole picture" we discussed in the beginning. Review the chart on pages 10 and 11. Also, remind your children that the Old Testament is the story of God dealing with mankind to prepare them for the coming of Christ. All that is recorded in these books are actual history. Every event points to the coming of Jesus, who saves us from our sins.

Leviticus is especially important because it highlights the "Holiness of God." Through all of the laws, offerings and feasts, we see how difficult it is for sinful man to approach a sinless God. Here are some thoughts for governing your discussions through the book:
1. God is very holy.
2. In order to approach God, we must walk in this kind of holiness.
3. It is impossible to be that good.
4. Jesus came and lived a "perfectly" holy life. Then, he became our sacrifice, priest, holy day and everything else.
5. If we put our trust in what Jesus did, we do not have to do anything in order to approach God.
6. If we have really received God's love and are His children, we are walking with Him and, therefore, His nature of holiness is working in us.

Special point to remember: The 10 commandments, Exodus 21, are 4 laws in regard to loving God and 6 in regard to loving our fellow man. The Laws of Leviticus are given to create a workable society for the health and well being of all involved. Although we are not bound to the Levitical Law as Christians, we must still become loving people who keep the ten commandments and observe the cultural practices that serves our God, family, church and fellow man.

Why don't we keep all the laws of Leviticus?
You will face the question, "Why don't we keep the feasts or the laws of Leviticus." The answer is very simple: "It certainly would not be wrong to keep them. Many of them were sanitation laws given for the protection of the society. With modern toilets, sanitation, and medical practices, we are better of to deal with societal norms differently.

One example is the manner in which the priests determined whether or not a person had leprosy. If a person had a sore that indicated the possibility of leprosy, the individual was quarantined and examined after seven days. If it were determined that the person had leprosy, they were removed from the camp.

The modern application of this would have the same result. A loving person with leprosy would not want to spread it. However, observation by a priest is not nearly so efficient as a modern test for leprosy. So, if a person has a spot that might indicate a communicable disease, the thing to do would be get a test immediately. The self-centered family, concerned only with their personal welfare, spread their germs around to everyone. Understanding the reason behind the laws should help us become more holy and loving. Whereas the application may change, from culture to culture, the eternal principle should always be followed.

Week 1: The five offerings

In advance, you should explain that there are five offerings. We will discuss one each day for a week. Each offering represents one aspect of our approach to a Holy God. The effect of understanding these laws of offerings should be to make your children: 1)appreciate that Jesus has become our offering, and 2)give them a desire to live a life of offering to the Lord.

Day 1
The Burnt Offering (Leviticus 1)

Purpose of today's lesson: To discover the "burnt offering," the reason for it and its affect on our relationship to God.

Why did the Israelites offer up the burnt offering and what were the results?

Explain (verse 4) that they offered up the burnt offering as an atonement. Also, show that the result was a soothing aroma unto the Lord (verse 17).

Day 2
The Grain Offering (Leviticus 2)

Purpose of today's lesson: To discover the "grain offering," the reason for it and its affect on a person's relationship to God.

Why did the Israelites offer the grain offering and what were the results?

Explain that the grain offering was used in conjunction with the Burnt or Peace offering. It brings the idea of offering "first fruits" (verse 12). It, too, becomes a sweet savor to the Lord (verse 9).

Day 3
The Peace Offering (Leviticus 3)

Purpose of today's lesson: To discover the "peace offering," it's reason and affects.

Why the peace offering?

Explain that the peace offering was used in ceremonies of family reunions, at the end of wars and completion of vows. Peace was very central to Israel's pursuit. By offering these types of offerings to the Lord, the acknowledged that God was their peace.

Day 4
The Sin Offering (Leviticus 4-5:13)

Purpose of today's lesson: To discover the Sin offering and it's purpose.

Why the Sin offering?

This one should be pretty simple (Verses 1 and 2). The result is just as simple (verse 35).

Day 5
The Trespass Offering (Leviticus 5:14-19-6:7)

Purpose of today's lesson: The same as the last four days, except for the Trespass Offering.

What is the Trespass offering? How is it different from the Sin Offering?

Explain that the Trespass offering was similar to the Sin Offering except for special circumstances (verses 14-17). Not only did the guilty party restore what he had defiled, he added 20 percent.

Week 2
The five offerings (part 2)

Day 1-2
Special commandments to the priests on the offerings. Leviticus 6 and 7

Purpose of today's lesson: To show how detailed the offering unto the Lord was. Not only were laws given about how the offering was to be brought, the priests were given special instructions on how to offer it.

Did God require the priests to do anything special at the different offerings?

Read the chapters and comment on the detail. The main idea is that God required strict obedience in every detail.

Day 3
Jesus is our Priest and Offering, in the tabernacle of heaven. Hebrews 7:11-10:18

Purpose of today's lesson: To show how Jesus became our offering.

How perfect did the offerings have to be?

Explain that Jesus was our offering to God. Emphasize Hebrews 9:6-28

Day 4
Jesus is our high priest (Hebrews 7-9)

Purpose of today's lesson: To recall the institution of priests and their special instructions in Leviticus 6-7. Then show how Christ is our priest and is much better.

Do you remember the special qualifications for priesthood and the way the priests were supposed to act?

Explain how Jesus was a much better priest than Aaron or any of his family. Emphasize Hebrews 7:11-28 (especially 22-28).

Day 5
The Tabernacle in Heaven (Hebrews 8:1-6 and 9:1-5,11)

Purpose of today's lesson: To review that Jesus ministered in the heavenly tabernacle of which the Tabernacle of Moses was only a type.

We studied the tabernacle of Moses. What did it represent?

Explain that the earthly tabernacle was only a type of what the tabernacle in heaven was like. Discuss how Jesus, as priest, gave himself as an offering, in the real and heavenly tabernacle.

Week 3
The preparation of priests - Leviticus 8-10

Day 1
The priests are set apart. Chapter 8

Purpose of today's lesson: To show how carefully the priests had to prepare before serving God.

Why did the priests have to be so careful? See v. 35

Read the chapter and comment on the detail. Explain that a priest cannot enter into God's presence with unconfessed sin. Ask your child if he or she could be worthy to go to God on behalf of a nation.

Day 2
The sacrifice of living animals to prepare the priests. Chapter 9

Purpose of today's lesson: To show how awesome God is in requiring death to atone for sin.

How many animals were sacrificed in preparing the priests?

Read through the chapter and count how many animals were sacrificed on this day.

Day 3
God is very specific in what offerings are acceptable. Chapter 10:1- 7

Purpose of today's lesson: To show how God cannot accept unholy offerings.

Only God knows what kind of sacrifice will really work. What if you try to offer something other than God's sacrifice to Him?

Read the chapter and explain how Nadab and Abihu offered "strange" fire.

Day 4 - Review Last Week to Shew Christ as the Perfect Priest

Day 5
The Tabernacle in Heaven Leviticus 10:9-11

Purpose of today's lesson: To discuss drinking with your children.

Why were the priests not allowed to drink wine or alcohol?

Explain that determining right and wrong, holy and unholy, could be affected if the priest were drunk. Coming before God required "sobriety of mind."

Week 4

As we move into the rest of Leviticus, we will be covering many different laws. Explain to your children that chapters 11 - 15 deal with health issues. Then, read a chapter a day to discover how God intended the children of Israel to conduct themselves in regard to personal hygiene and public health.

For each day:

Read a chapter.
See what particular law catches your child's attention.
Try to discover why God would have them keep this particular law.

Once again, your children will want to know why we do not keep all of these laws. The answer is very simple. These laws were given to keep God's children safe in the environment where they lived. Because of modern technology, many of the health threats can be dealt with in a different way. However, some of the practices are still beneficial for health reasons.

Day 1-Chapter 11- Laws about Animals for Food.

Day 2-Chapter 12- Laws of motherhood. You may use this time to explain some things about birth and the health hazards associated with birth. Fathers, you can mention the great sacrifice of mothers in birthing children.

Day 3- Chapter 13 & 14- Testing and Cleansing for Leprosy.

Day 4- Chapter 15- This should be interesting. I would love to know what you share with your children about this!!!

Day 5- Chapter 16 & 17- Discuss the atonement with your children. Refer to Hebrews 9 & 10 and discuss the parallel between Jesus as a sacrifice and the atonement.

I want to apologize for the notes being sketchy this week. You will have to do a little more work yourself.

NUMBERS

I. Week 1 God Numbers the People (Num 1 - 4)

Day 1
The men of war (Num 1:1-46)

The purpose of today's lesson: God is intimately involved in the
affairs of His people.

Why would God have Moses number the men of war?

Explain that God wanted the people to know that He was a part of their
everyday lives.

Day 2
The Levites are separated (Num 1:47 - 54)

The purpose of today's lesson: God will always have a people to
worship Him.

What was the reason God separated the Levites from the rest of the
people?

Explain that God will always have a priesthood and what the purpose of
that priesthood is.

Day 3
God sets up the camp (Num 2)

The purpose of today's lesson: God is involved with the structure of
His people to get His purposes accomplished.

Why was God interested in the structure of the camp?

Explain how God structures life to accomplish His purpose.

Day 4
The Levites, the first born unto the Lord (Num 3 - 4)

The purpose of today's lesson: God reserve the best (first born) for
    Himself.

What is the first born?

Explain the concept of the first born as it pertains to the offerings, the
    Levites and Jesus.

Day 5
The duties of the Levites (Num 3 - 4)

The purpose of today's lesson: The priesthood unto God has
    defined responsibilities.

What were the responsibilities of the Levites?

Explain the responsibilities of the Levites.

II. Week 2 The Lord Sanctifies Israel (Num 5 - 10:10)

Day 1
The Law (Num 5)

The purpose of today's lesson: God used the Law to separate the
    people to Himself.

What laws were restated to the people to help them walk with God?

Review how God gives us the Law to show us who He is and how we
    should walk.

Day 2
The Nazarite (Num 6, Judges 13 - 16)

The purpose of today's lesson: To show that there are special
    callings to come away unto God for His service.

What were the special qualifications of the Nazarite and who was the
    most well known Nazarite?

Discuss the qualifications of the Nazarite and talk about the life of
　　Samson.

Day 3
The Offerings (Num 7 - 8)

The purpose of today's lesson: Show how God uses offerings to
　　sanctify His people.

What were some offerings that God restated at this time?

Review some of the offerings and discuss why these offerings were done.

Day 4
Feasts (Num 9:1 - 14)

The purpose of today's lesson: God used the feasts to remind
　　people of who He and they are.

Why did God remind them of the Passover?

Discuss the Passover and the importance of that feast.

Day 5
Divine guidance (Num 9:15 - 10:10)

The purpose of today's lesson: God will guide His people in their
　　lives.

How did God guide His people in their journeys?

Discuss how God lead the people with the cloud.

III. Week 3 The Journey to Kadesh (Num 10:11 - 12)

Day 1
The people complain (Num 10:11 - 11:9)

The purpose of today's lesson: During difficult times people will
　　frequently turn to the flesh instead of trusting God.

What was Israel's response to difficult times?

Discuss what the people did during this tough time.

Day 2
Moses complains about the people (Num 11:10 - 15)

The purpose of today's lesson: Leaders, in the flesh, blame the
people.

What was Moses' response to the rebellion of the people?

Discuss what Moses did when the people complained.

Day 3
God provides for Moses (Num 11:16 - 30)

The purpose of today's lesson: God's gracious response to His
leaders.

What did God do in response to Moses?

Discuss God's response to Moses

Day 4
God provides for the people (Num 11:31 - 35)

The purpose of today's lesson: See God's response to a rebellious
people.

What did God do in response to the complaints of Israel?

Tell what God does when His people complain.

Day 5
Aaron and Mariam (Num 12)

The purpose of today's lesson: See what can happen when people
speak against God's man.

What was the complaint of Mariam and Aaron and what did God do?

Tell the story of Mariam and Aaron and God's response.

IV. Week 4 Israel at Kadesh (Num 13 - 14)

Day 1
Spies in the land (Num 13:1 - 33)

The purpose of today's lesson: Show the wonderful promise God
        prepared for His people.

What did the spies find in the land?

Discuss the wonderful promise land.

Day 2
Rebellion despite the promise. (Num 14:1 - 10)

The purpose of today's lesson: People frequently see only the
        down side.

What did the people do after the report of the spies?

Tell the story of Israel's response to the spies.

Day 3
Moses intercedes for the people (Num 14:11 - 19)

The purpose of today's lesson: Show what a leader should do
        when the people go wrong.

What did Moses do and say when the people came against God?

Continue the story about Israel's response and what Moses did.

Day 4
The judgment of God (Num 14:20 - 38)

The purpose of today's lesson: One way God responds to rebellion.

What did God do to Israel?

Continue the story with God's response.

Day 5
Israel rejects God's judgment (Num 14:39 - 45)

The purpose of today's lesson: Show that people rebel even after
    God judges.

What was Israel's response to God's judgment?

Continue the story emphasizing how judgment does not always bring
    repentance.

V. Week 5 Israel in the Wilderness (Num 15 - 19)

Day 1
Review of the offerings (Num 15)

The purpose of today's lesson: Holiness is important to God.

What was Israel to do when it entered the land?

Tell how God emphasizes holiness as shown in His offerings.

Day 2
The rebellion of Korah (Num 16:1 - 40)

The purpose of today's lesson: People throughout the ages have
    accused leaders and God defends the leaders.

What was the accusation of Korah? Moses' response? God's response?

Tell the story of Korah emphasizing Moses' response and God's
    response.

Day 3
Israel comes against Moses and Aaron (Num 16:41 - 50)

The purpose of today's lesson: Frequently the people take the
    wrong side when things happen.

After the judgment of Korah, what did Israel do?

Continue the story with what Israel did emphasizing what God did and
    what Moses did.

Day 4
Aaron's rod buds (Num 17)

The purpose of today's lesson: God selects His leadership.

How was Aaron chosen?

Tell the story of the selection of Aaron as high priest.

Day 5
The duties of the priesthood (Num 18 - 19)

The purpose of today's lesson: The things that God values are
      repeated.

Why were the duties of the priesthood repeated?

Show them that God repeats those things that are important.

VI. Travel to Moab (Num 20 - 25)

Day 1
Water from the rock (Num 20:1 - 13)

The purpose of today's lesson: Show an example of a lack of faith.

What was wrong with Moses hitting the rock twice?

Tell the story about the rock emphasizing Moses hit the rock twice.

Day 2
The fiery serpents (Num 20:14 - 21:9; John 3:14)

The purpose of today's lesson: The meaning of the bronze serpent.

What is the importance of the bronze serpent?

Tell the story of the travels through Edom and the fiery serpents showing
      Jesus as our bronze serpent.

Day 3
Balaam hears from God (Num 21:10 - 22:41)

The purpose of today's lesson: Show how God will get His
purposes done anyway He can.

How did God speak to Moses?

Tell the story of God speaking to Balaam.

Day 4
Balaam can't be bought. (Num 23 -24)

The purpose of today's lesson: Show that Balaam did not sell his
prophecy.

Why didn't Balaam do what Balak wanted?

Tell the story of Balaam and Balak.

Day 5
Phinehas preserves righteousness (Num 25)

The purpose of today's lesson: Show that zeal for God is rewarded.

Why did God commend Phinehas for killing people?

Tell the story of chapter 25 discussing what Phinehas did.

VII. Week 7 Israel in a New Land (Num 26 - 31)

Day 1
God takes a second census (Num 26)

The purpose of today's lesson: Show that God is continually
involved in the details.

Why did God take another census?

Re-emphasize God's involvement with details.

Day 2
Rules of inheritance (Num 27)

The purpose of today's lesson: Show the fair handling of
inheritance.

What are the rules for inheritance?

Go over how property was inherited.

Day 3
Review of the offerings (Num 28 - 29)

The purpose of today's lesson: In the new situation God reviews the
basics.

Why did God review the offerings?

Discuss the offerings emphasizing God reviewing the basics.

Day 4
Vows (Num 30)

The purpose of today's lesson: Show the binding nature of our
word.

What were the rules regarding vows?

Review these rules emphasizing the binding nature of our word.

Day 5
Israel destroys Midian (Num 31)

The purpose of today's lesson: Show that God has no place for see
amongst His people.

Why was Israel to destroy Midian completely?

Explain that God does not allow any part of the flesh to survive.

VIII. Week 8 Israel in a New Land (Num 32 - 36)

Day 1
Division of the Land East of Jordan (Num 32)

The purpose of today's lesson: To learn the proper priorities of life.

What was the purpose of making sure Reuben and Gad joined in the
        fight?

Tell the story about Reuben and Gad emphasizing the proper priority of
        God first, others second and selfish interests third.

Day 2
The Summary of Israel's Journey (Num 33:1 - 49)

The purpose of today's lesson: God is with us through all our
        journeys in life.

Why would God review the journey of Israel?

Briefly review the journey of Israel emphasizing God's care for His people.

Day 3
The Division of the Land (Num 33:50 - 34:29)

The purpose of today's lesson: God provides the inheritance to His
        people.

Why did God specifically divide the land and set the leadership?

Talk about the division of the land telling that God want there to be no
        division over how the land was taken care of.

Day 4
Cities of Safety (Num 35)

The purpose of today's lesson: God provides places of refuge for
        the just.

What was the functions of the cities of refuge?

Talk about the law concerning the cities of refuge telling about how God provides refuge for the faithful.

Day 5
Keeping the Inheritance within the Tribe (Num 36)

The purpose of today's lesson: Show that God wanted the inheritance to remain as He planned it.

Why did God make these rules about the inheritance?

Review the special rules of inheritance showing that God's rules protect us all.

IX. Week 9 Review of Numbers

Day 1
The Preparation of the Journey (Num 1 - 10)

The purpose of today's lesson: To review how God prepares His people for their journeys.

Can you think of a time God prepared you for a journey?

Review the first ten chapters showing that God prepares His people for the journeys of life.

Day 2
The Wilderness Wanderings (Num 11 - 20)

The purpose of today's lesson: Our wanderings in the wilderness shows us what manner of people we are.

Has God ever shown you your heart? Describe.

Review the following showing how God reveals the heart of the people: the people complaining, Aaron and Mariam, Korah, spies in the land.

Day 3
The Journey to Canaan (Num 21 - 36)

The purpose of today's lesson: Review the entry of the people into the land and its effect on us.

Can you recall a time when you did an unpopular thing because God told you to?

Review the fiery serpents, the life of Balaam, Phinehas with its effect in our lives.

Day 4
Numbers in Your Life

The purpose of today's lesson: Application of scripture to your life

What is your favorite story in Numbers and why?

Help your children pick a story from Numbers and talk about it.

Day 5
Numbers in Your Life

The purpose of today's lesson: Application of scripture to your life.

Who is your favorite person in Numbers and why?

Help your children pick a character from Numbers and talk about it.

JOSHUA

I. Week 1 The preparation of the people (Joshua 1 - 5)

A. Day 1
The call of Joshua (Joshua 1:1-18)

The purpose of today's lesson: God calls each of His leaders specifically.

Why did God talk to Joshua the way He did?

Tell the story of the call of Joshua emphasizing how special it was since Joshua was replacing Moses.

B. Day 2
Rahab hides the spies (Joshua 2:1 - 24)

The purpose of today's lesson: God uses unexpected people to perform His works.

Who was Rahab and how did God use her to conquer Jericho?

Tell the story of Rahab and the spies emphasizing how God uses anyone to perform His will.

C. Day 3
Israel enters the land (Joshua 3:1 - 17)

The purpose of today's lesson: God leads His people into the Promised Land.

Why did the ark go in first?

Describe Israel coming into the land.

D. Day 4
Twelve stones (Joshua 4:1 – 24)

The purpose of today's lesson: God wants His people to remember when He moves in their lives.

What was the purpose of the twelve stones?

Discuss the memorial built to commemorate God bringing Israel into the land.

E. Day 5
Joshua prepares Israel spiritually (Joshua 5:1 – 15)

The purpose of today's lesson: Before doing God's work, one must be prepared in his heart.

What did Joshua do prior to invading Jericho?

Discuss what Joshua did and whom he met with.

II. Week 2 Conquest (Joshua 6 - 11)

A. Day 1
Jericho (Joshua 6:1 - 27)

The purpose of today's lesson: God's conquest comes God's way

How did Israel conquer Jericho?

Tell the story of the conquest of Jericho.

B. Day 2
Ai (Joshua 7:1 – 8:35)

The purpose of today's lesson: God's judgement is sure.

Why did Israel lose at Ai?

Tell the story of Ai emphasizing the transgression of Achan.

C. Day 3
Gibeon (Joshua 9:1 – 27)

The purpose of today's lesson: Make no covenants without the direction of God.

How did the Gibeonites trick Joshua?

Tell the story of Gibeon emphasizing the treachery of Gibeon.

D. Day 4
The day the sun stood still (Joshua 10:1 - 28)

The purpose of today's lesson: **Nature listens to the man of God doing the will of God.**

What miraculous event occurred when Joshua fought the five kings?

Tell the story of the battle against the five kings emphasizing two points: the sun stood still for Joshua and Joshua destroyed everything in victory.

E. Day 5
No survivors (Joshua 10:29 –11:23, II Cor 5:17)

The purpose of today's lesson: **When God removes the old and replaces it with the new, the old is destroyed completely.**

Why did Joshua kill everybody?

Tell the story of the further conquests emphasizing the destruction of everyone and relating that to how we must deal with sin in our lives.

III. Week 3 Settlement (Joshua 12 - 20)

A. Day 1
The summary of the conquest (Joshua 12:1 – 24)

The purpose of today's lesson: **God continually reviews His actions in the lives of His people.**

Why did God review the conquest?

Go over the summary of the conquests discussing God's principle of His people remembering His action in their lives.

B. Day 2
Inheritance of Reuben, Gad and ½ Manasseh (Joshua 13:1 – 33, Num 32:1 – 6, Joshua 1:12 - 18)

<u>The purpose of today's lesson</u>: God keeps His promises.

What was the deal these tribes made with Moses?

Discuss the inheritance of these tribes highlighting their covenant with God.

C. Day 3
Caleb (Joshua 14:1 – 15, 15:13 - 19, Numbers 13 & 14)

<u>The purpose of today's lesson</u>: God never forgets the righteous man.

Who was Caleb?

Review the story of the life of Caleb.

D. Day 4
The settlement of the land (Joshua 15:1 – 12, 15:19 – 19:51)

<u>The purpose of today's lesson</u>: **God divides up the land just as He arranged the camp and was involved in many other details of the life of Israel.**

How was the land divided?

Discuss the settlement of the land making sure to mention the division by lot.

E. Day 5
Cities of refuge (Joshua 20:1 – 9)

<u>The purpose of today's lesson</u>: God makes provision to avoid **unnecessary judgement.**

What are cities of refuge?

Discuss cities of refuge and their purpose.

IV. Week 4 Israel in the Land (Joshua 21 - 24)

A. Day 1
Settlement of Levi (Joshua 21:1 – 45)

The purpose of today's lesson: The people care for their priests.

How did Levi obtain its settlement?

Tell the story of how each tribe gave to provide for Levi.

B. Day 2
The altar, "Witness". (Joshua 22:1 - 34)

The purpose of today's lesson: God recognizes proper motives.

Why did Reuben and Gad build the altar?

Tell the story of the altar, "Witness".

C. Day 3
Remain faithful to God (Joshua 23:1 - 16)

The purpose of today's lesson: The most important thing for God's people is to remain faithful to God.

What was Joshua's advice the people after the wars were over?

Tell the story after the end of the wars stressing remaining faithful to God.

D. Day 4
The covenant re-affirmed (Joshua 24:1 - 27)

The purpose of today's lesson: God repeatedly re-affirms the people's commitment to Him.

Why did Joshua re-write the covenant and peoples' commitment to it?

Discuss the review of the history of Israel and re-affirmation of their covenant to God.

E. Day 5
Joshua dies (Joshua 24:28 - 33)

The purpose of today's lesson: The people followed God under Joshua's wise leadership.

Did the people continue to serve the Lord even after Joshua's death?

Discuss how the people followed God even after Joshua died as a result of his wise leadership.

V. Week 5 Joshua in Review (Joshua 1 - 24)

A. Day 1
The Call of Joshua

The purpose of today's lesson: Leaders must start with God's call.

What did Joshua receive before he started leading Israel?

Review the call of God on the life of Joshua.

B. Day 2
Conquest

The purpose of today's lesson: God will go before a people who follow Him.

Why did Israel always win their battles no matter the odds?

Review all the battles showing God's faithfulness.

C. Day 3
No survivors

The purpose of today's lesson: God wants His people purged of all evil.

Why did God require everyone in the conquered cities be destroyed?

Review this principle stressing the need for personal purity.

D. Day 4
Settlement

The purpose of today's lesson: God divided the land according to a detailed plan.

How was the land divided up especially for Levi, Reuben, Gad and ½ Manasseh?

Review the division of the land.

E. Day 5
Covenant

The purpose of today's lesson: God re-affirms the covenant at significant points in history,

Why did God have the people re-commit to Him?

Discuss the principle of re-commitment and why it was done at this time.

Billy Henderson

JUDGES

Week 1 Israel Fails in Conquest (Judges 1)

Day 1
Judah defeats Canaan (Judges 1:1 - 11)

The purpose of today's lesson: God's calling was to utterly destroy the men of Canaan.

What was God's command regarding how Israel should conquer Canaan?

Review God's command to defeat Canaan and how that relates to our lives.

Day 2
Caleb and Achsah (Judges 1:12 – 15)

The purpose of today's lesson: Caleb's relationship to his daughter.

What was Caleb's relationship to his daughter?

Explain how Caleb gave his daughter her desire.

Day 3
Israel fails to destroy the inhabitants (Judges 1:16 – 36)

The purpose of today's lesson: Compromise of God's standard creeps into the camp.

What did Israel allow to happen in the conquest of Canaan?

Tell the story of conquest emphasizing (as the text does) that all the inhabitants were not destroyed.

Day 4
Forced labor (Judges 1:28 – 36)

The purpose of today's lesson: Israel justifies compromise.

What did Israel do with the inhabitants they did not destroy?

Discuss what Israel did instead of destroying the enemy and how that was wrong.

Day 5
Application (Judges 1:1 – 36)

The purpose of today's lesson: Use this day to make application of what happened in history ("Those who fail to study history are destined to repeat it")

What is one or two ways that you may compromise God's commands in you life?

Assist the children in thinking of ways they have possibly compromised God's commands or could possibly compromise.

Week 2 The Results of Compromise (Judges 2 – 3:8)

Day 1
The angel of the Lord (Judges 2:1 – 3)

The purpose of today's lesson: God speaks the results of compromise.

What did the angel of the Lord say when he visited Israel?

Discuss the appearance of the angel of the Lord and what he said.

Day 2
Israel's response to the proclamation of judgement.

The purpose of today's lesson: Proper response to God's proclamation.

What was Israel's response to the angel of the Lord?

Discuss Israel's response and how that was proper.

Day 3
Last days of Joshua

The purpose of today's lesson: Israel did well as long as Joshua was alive

How did the people behave as long as Joshua was alive?

Discuss the last days of Joshua emphasizing that Israel did well until he died.

Day 4
They did not know the Lord

The purpose of today's lesson: When people do not know God they sin,

What happened once the people did not know God?

Discuss the times after Joshua's death.

Day 5
Israel does what is evil in the sight of the Lord

The purpose of today's lesson: To see the relationship between God and a people who do not know Him.

What was the relationship between God and Israel?

Tell about these times emphasizing that this was a people that did not know God.

Week 3 Early Judges (Judges 3:9-5:31)

Day 1
Othniel (Judges 3:9-11)

The purpose of today's lesson: God raised a deliverer in response to prayer

Who was Othniel and why did he rise up

Give a story of Othniel's life especially how God raised him up as a deliverer.

Day 2
Ehud (Judges 3:12-30)

The purpose of today's lesson: God has a sense of humor

What was special about Eglon the king?

Tell the story of Ehud and Eglon.

Day 3
Shamgar (Judges 3:31)

The purpose of today's lesson: The Philistines become and important enemy.

Who is the enemy that Shamgar defeats?

This is the first mention of an important enemy of Israel thoughout their history.

Day 4 & 5 (Judges 4:1-5:31)
Deborah and Barak

The purpose of today's lesson: Under wise leadership Israel prevails

Did Israel prosper under the leadership of Deborah and Barak?

Give they story of Deborah and Barak.

Week 4 Gideon (Judges 6:1-8:32)

Day 1
The sins of Israel (Judges 6:1-10)

The purpose of today's lesson: As soon as they are left on their own, the people turn away from God.

After Deborah died what happened to Israel?

Tell about how Israel sinned and was conquered by Midian.

Day 2
The call of Gideon (Judges 6:11-40)

The purpose of today's lesson: God always uses the meek.

What was Gideon doing when he was called?

Tell the story of the call of Gideon.

Day 3 & 4
Midian is defeated (Judges 7:1-8:21)

The purpose of today's lesson: When God raises up a man they are victorious

What happened once Gideon took over?

Discuss the defeat of Midian emphasizing God's part.

Day 5
Gideon judges (Judges 8:22-35)

<u>The purpose of today's lesson:</u> **God will rule over you.**

What did Gideon say when the people asked him to rule?

Discuss the rule of Gideon and what happened after he died.

Week 5 Between Gideon and Samson (Judges 9:1-12:15)

Day 1
Abimelech (Judges 9)

<u>The purpose of today's lesson:</u> **To see how things went between the rule of Gideon and Samson.**

What did Abimelech have to deal with during his rule?

Discuss the time of Abimelech especially how people did not want to follow him.

Day 2
Tola and Jair (Judges 10)

<u>The purpose of today's lesson:</u> **Again Israel followed God as long as they had a leader.**

What happened after Jair died and why?

Discuss the rule of these two men and how Israel did well as long as they had a ruler.

Day 3 & 4
Jephthah (Judges 11:1-12:7)

<u>The purpose of today's lesson:</u> **God can use any man. Make no idle promise.**

Why was Jephthah initially shunned? What promise did he make that he regretted?

Tell the story of Jephthah discussing his origins and his promise.

Day 5
Ibzon, Elon, Abdon (12:8-15)

Who were the three Judges between Samson and Jephthah?

Review these three judges.

Week 6 Samson (Judges 13:1-16:31)

Day 1
The birth of Samson, the Nazorite (Judges 13)

The purpose of today's lesson: Review the miraculous birth of Samson.

What was special about the birth and calling of Samson?

Tell the story of Samson's birth reviewing the vows of a Nazirite.

Day 2
Samson's marriage (Judges 14)

The purpose of today's lesson: Even men called of God make foolish choices.

What was wrong with Samson's choice of a wife?

Tell the story of Samson's marriage.

Day 3
Samson's rule (Judges 15)

The purpose of today's lesson: Review the very successful rule of Samson.

Despite his mistakes, was Samson's rule a good one in Israel?

Review the successful rule of Samson.

Day 4
Samson's fall (Judges 16:1-22)

The purpose of today's lesson: Show that old weaknesses can hurt us if not removed.

Why did Samson fall?

Tell the story of Samson and Delilah emphasizing Samson's weakness for women.

Day 5
Samson's deliverance (Judges 16:23-31)

The purpose of today's lesson: Even when we fall on our face God does not forsake us.

Ultimately did God come back to help Samson?

Discuss the death of Samson highlighting Judges 16:28.

Week 7 Depravity of Israel (Judges 17:1-21:25)

Day 1
Personal idolatry (Judges 17)

The purpose of today's lesson: There was no king and every man did what was right in his own eyes.

What did they make from the silver?

Tell the story of Micah.

Day 2
Tribal idolatry (Judges 18)

The purpose of today's lesson: Personal idolatry will spread to the people.

What did the tribe of Dan steal from Micah?

Discuss the story of chapter 18 and how they stole idols.

Day 3
Personal immorality (Judges 19:1-10)

The purpose of today's lesson: Without a king, immorality follows idolatry

Why were the people not faithful to their married relationships?

Tell this story with an eye toward the development of personal infidelity.

Day 4
Tribal immorality (19:11-30)

The purpose of today's lesson: As with idolatry immorality spreads to others.

What happened to the woman?

Tell the remainder of the story.

Day 5
Failure in relationship (Judges 20:1-21:25)

The purpose of today's lesson: As life in Israel fell apart, the people ultimately came to war.

What was the ultimate result of the death of the woman?

Discuss how immorality led to war.

Week 8 Review of Judges (Judges)

Day 1
The people sin without a leader

The purpose of today's lesson: Review how the people consistently turned from God when the leaders died.

Every time the people were without a leader what did they do?

Review what happened when Joshua died and when each judge died.

Day 2
Gideon

The purpose of today's lesson: God can use anyone regardless of his or her own gifts.

What sort of man was Gideon when God called him?

Review Gideon's character and how God used him despite himself.

Day 3
Jephthah

<u>**The purpose of today's lesson:**</u> **Idle words can lead to great pain.**

What happened to Jephthah's daughter?

Retell the story of Jephthah.

Day 4
Samson

<u>**The purpose of today's lesson:**</u> **small things can overcome Great men.**

What was Samson's greatest weakness?

Review the life of Samson.

Day 5
Depravity

<u>**The purpose of today's lesson:**</u> **People without God end up in despair.**

What things went on in Israel after Samson died?

Review Israel's history after Samson died high-lighting these were people without a leader.

I Samuel

I. **Week 1 Birth of Samuel (I Sam 1:1-2:17)**

Day 1 (I Sam 1:1-11)
Hannah's vow

The purpose of today's lesson: When we turn to God in desperation He will answer.

Why did Hannah make a promise to God?

Talk about Hannah and her promise to God.

Day 2 (I Sam 1:12-18)
Hannah's desperation

The purpose of today's lesson: True faith comes from exhausting of man's answers.

Why was Hannah so desperate?

Go over Hannah's life with an emphasis on how her anxiety lead to faith.

Day 3 (I Sam 1:19-28)
The Lord answers Hannah

The purpose of today's lesson: God answers the prayer of desperate faith.

What was God's response to Hannah?

Tell what God did in response to Hannah's vow.

Day 4 (I Sam 2:1-10)
Hannah's praise

The purpose of today's lesson: When God meets us our response is praise.

What did Hannah do after God met her?

Go over Hannah's praise showing that she gave God all the credit.

Day 5 (I Sam 2:11-17)
The sin of Eli and his sons

The purpose of today's lesson: When fathers don't lead sons fall into sin.

Why were Eli's sons so bad?

Tell the story of Eli's sons showing that their sin was a result of their own wickedness and Eli's failure to lead.

II. Week 2 From Eli to Samuel (I Sam 2:18-3:21)

Day 1 (I Sam 2:18-25)
Israel needs new leadership

The purpose of today's lesson: Show the need for new leadership.

What was the state of leadership in Israel at this time?

Tell the story of how things were when Samuel was born.

Day 2 (I Sam 2:26-36)
God's response to unrighteous leadership.

The purpose of today's lesson: Show that God will raise up Godly leadership in the midst of depravity.

Why was Samuel raised up?

Discuss God's response to Eli's sons.

Day 3 (I Sam 3:1-10)
Speak Lord, your servant hears

The purpose of today's lesson: Know the appropriate response to God's call.

What was Samuel's response once he knew it weas God?

Tell this story emphasizing, God speaks to children, and the right answer.

Day 4 (I Sam 3:11-18)
God calls Samuel

The purpose of today's lesson: God call can come to children.

What did God tell Samuel?

Go over this scripture showing that God can call children.

Day 5 (I Sam 3:19-21)
Samuel grows strong.

The purpose of today's lesson: God accomplishes His work.

What happens to Samuel at this point?

Continue the story emphasizing God's faithfulness.

III. Week 3 Israel is Defeated (I Sam 4-6)

A. Day 1 (I Sam 4:1-11)
Israel is defeated

The purpose of today's lesson: Israel faced a powerful enemy.

What happened Israel when they faced the Philistines?

Tell the story of this portion of scripture emphasizing the victory of the Philistines over Israel.

B. Day 2 (I Sam 4:12-18)
The death of Eli

The purpose of today's lesson: Men who do not follow God die untimely deaths.

Why did Eli die?

Tell the story of Eli's death emphasizing the untimely nature of his death.

C. Day 3 (I Sam 4:19-22)
Ichabod

The purpose of today's lesson: **People mourn the loss of God's presence.**

Why did the woman name her child Ichabod?

Tell the story of Ichabod birth showing that people mourn when God's presence is lost.

D. Day 4 (I Sam 5)
Ashdod

The purpose of today's lesson: **The ungodly cannot deal with the presence of God.**

What happened to Ashdod when it stole the Ark of God?

Read chapter 5 showing that the presence of God in a heathen place lead to judgment.

E. Day 5 (I Sam 6)
The Philistines with the Ark

The purpose of today's lesson: more information regarding the problems that the pagans experience with the presence of God.

What happened to the Philistines when they had the Ark?

Tell the story of chapter 6 showing that these people could not work with the presence of God.

IV. Week 4 Victories under Samuel and the Call for a King (I Sam 7, 8)

Day 1
Samuel's Promise (I Sam 7:1-4)

The purpose of today's lesson: God calls his people to serve him on.

What was the condition for Israel's victory?

Explain how Samuel promised victory as long as the people did not serve other gods.

Day 2
Israel defeats the Philistines at Mispah (I Sam 7:5-12)

The purpose of today's lesson: When Israel follow God their enemies were defeated.

Why did Israel win this battle?

Explain the next victory showing that Israel won because they were devoted to the Lord.

Day 3
Israel continued in victory under Samuel (I Sam 7:13-17)

To purpose of today's lesson: To show that victory continued while they followed the man of God.

How did things go for Israel in the subsequent years?

Show that victory continued under Samuel's reign.

Day 4
Call for a king (I Sam 8:1-11)

In the purpose of today's lesson: When there is no leader the people will demand one.

What are two reasons Israel demanded a king?

Tell the story of this chapter showing why Israel wanted a king.

Day 5
The Problem with the King (I Sam 8:12-22)

The purpose of today's lesson: Show was wrong with an earthly king.

Why is it not necessarily good to have a king?

Show the problems Israel faced with a king.

V.   Week 5 Saul Is Chosen As King (I Sam 9, 10)

Day 1
Beautiful to behold (I Sam 9:1-2)

The purpose of today's lesson: People choose leaders by how they look.

Why was Saul chosen as king?

Tell why Saul was chosen as king.

Day 2
Saul meets Samuel (I Sam 9:3-27)

The purpose of today's lesson: God speaks to his leaders in advance.

How did Samuel that Saul was to be king?

Tell the story of these verses emphasizing that Samuel knew that Saul was to be the king.

Day 3
Saul is anointed king (I Sam 10:1-9)

The purpose of today's lesson: Samuel obeys God and gives Israel a king.

What did Samuel do despite knowing the trouble it would cause?

Tell how Samuel anointed Saul and gave him direction despite knowing the problems that would occur.

Day 4
Saul visits the prophets (I Sam 10:10-16)

<u>The purpose of today's lesson</u>: When Saul obeyed Samuel he was blessed.

What happened to Saul when he visited the prophets?

Show that when Saul visited the prophets he was blessed by God.

Day 5
Saul is presented to the people (I Sam 10:17-27)

<u>The purpose of today's lesson</u>: God will give you what you want even when it's not good for you.

Was God happy about Israel's desire for king?

Discuss the story of the presentation of Saul showing that God gave them a king even though he didn't want them to have one.

VI. Week 6 Saul's Early Reign (I Samuel 11-13)

Day 1
Saul at War (I Samuel 11)

The Purpose of Today's Lesson: See command go from Samuel to Saul.

Why did Saul kill the oxen?

Tell the story of this chapter describing how Saul motivated the people.

Day 2
Samuel Steps Down (I Samuel 12)

The Purpose of Today's Lesson: Understand last act of a great leader.

What was Samuel's main warning to the people?

Discussed when Samuel steps down as the leader of the people and his main message to the people.

Day 3
Jonathan Starts the War (I Samuel 13:1-4)

The Purpose of Today's Lesson: See how easily animosity start.

Why did the war start between the Philistines and Israel?

Discuss the start of a war and how easily it began.

Day 4
Saul Offers a Sacrifice (I Samuel 13:5-14)

The Purpose of Today's Lesson: Obedience is better than sacrifice.

Why was it wrong for Saul to make the sacrifice?

Discuss the story showing the importance of obedience.

Day 5
Fighting without Weapons (I Samuel 13:15-23)

The Purpose of Today's Lesson: See how to respond to difficulty.

What happened to all the weapons?

Tell this story showing how Israel responds to the lack of weapons.

VII. Week 7 David, Jonathan and Saul (I Sam 14

Day 1
Jonathan slaughters the Phillistines (I Sam 14:1-15)

The Purpose of Today's Lesson: Hear from God and win the day.

Why did Jonathan win?

Tell this story emphasizing Jonathan heard from God.

Day 2
Israel follows Jonathan's lead (I Sam 14:16-23)

The Purpose of Today's Lesson: People will follow the amn of God as he follows God.

What inspired the people to victory?

Tell how Jonathan's faith encouraged the nation.

Day 3
Jonathan shows Saul the way of the Lord (I Sam 14:24-52)

The Purpose of Today's Lesson: The word of God is not always sacrefice.

Who was right, Jonathan or Saul? Why?

Tell how Saul was wrong to fast and Jonathan right to eat.

Day 4
I feared the people (I Sam 15)

The Purpose of Today's Lesson: It is better to obey God despite what people think.

Why did Saul spare the animals and Agag and why was it wrong?

Tell of the conquest of the Amalekites and Saul's mistake.

Day 5
The cost of disobedience (I Sam 15)

<u>The Purpose of Today's Lesson</u>: **See the terrible cost of disobedience**

What was the result of Saul's disobedience?

Discuss the price of Saul's rebellion and why God was so strict.

VIII. Week 8 God Chooses a New King (I Sam 16 - 17)

Day 1
David is chosen (I Sam 16:1-13)

The purpose of today's lesson: God is not looking at the outward appearance.

Why was David chosen and his brothers not chosen?

Tell the story of the selection of David emphasizing that Samuel wanted to pick his brothers because they were better looking but God chose David because of his heart.

Day 2
David comforts Saul (I Sam 16:14-23)

The purpose of today's lesson: God moves his people into places of importance.

Why did David play for Saul?

Tell how David ended up in Saul's court.

Day 3
Goliath challenges Israel (I Sam 17: 1-11)

The purpose of today's lesson: The challenges of life can appear insurmountable.

Describe Goliath.

Review this portion of scripture emphasizing the hopeless nature of fighting Goliath.

Day 4
David volunteers to fight Goliath (I Sam 17: 12-37)

The purpose of today's lesson: To see how a Godly man approaches the challenges of life.

Why did David feel he could defeat Goliath?

Tell how David volunteered to fight Goliath emphasizing his faith in God.

Day 5
David defeats Goliath (I Sam 17: 38-58)

The purpose of today's lesson: God fights for those who trust in him.

Why did David defeat Goliath?

Tell how David won the fight telling how God helped him win.

IX. Week 9 Saul Hates David (I Sam 18 – 19)

Day 1
Jonathan loves David (I Sam 18:1-4)

The purpose of today's lesson: See a committed relationship between two men.

What was the relationship between Jonathan and David?

Describe the relationship between Jonathan and David.

Day 2
Saul tries to kill David (I Sam 18: 5-30)

The purpose of today's lesson: Jealousy can destroy a man.

Why did Saul hate David?

Tell the story of this portion of scripture highlighting Saul's jealousy for David.

Day 3
Jonathan helps David (I Sam 19: 1-7)

The purpose of today's lesson: Covenant can be deeper than family commitments.

Why did Jonathan, Saul's son, help David?

Explain to your child how covenant commitments are deeper than family in some cases.

Day 4
Saul again tries to kill David (I Sam 19: 8-17)

<u>The purpose of today's lesson</u>: **Jealousy can blind you completely.**

After David fought for Saul, what did Saul do as a reward?

Explain Saul's second attempt on David life and how jealousy had completely blinded him.

Day 5
David flees from Saul (I Sam 19: 18-24)

<u>The purpose of today's lesson</u>: **God does everything to prevent us from going astray.**

Why does God continued to move in Saul's life?

Tell about Saul's visit to the prophets and how God spoke to him there.

X. Week 10 David Flees from Saul (I Sam 20 – 22)

Day 1
Jonathan helps David (I Sam 20:1-23)

The purpose of today's lesson: To expand on the relationship between David and Jonathan.

Why did Jonathan offer to help David?

Tell about Jonathan's plan to help David and the renewal of covenant.

Day 2
Saul seeks to kill David (I Sam 20:24-42)

The purpose of today's lesson: Show Jonathan's relationship with David is stronger than with Saul, his father.

Did Jonathan help David? How?

Tell the remainder of the story focusing on how Jonathan was true to David.

Day 3
The priests help David (I Sam 21:1-9)

The purpose of today's lesson: When we don't trust it hurts others around us.

Why was it bad for David to seek help from the priests?

Tell this story revealing that there are grave consequences for the priests.

Day 4
David goes to the Philistines (I Sam 21:10-15)

The purpose of today's lesson: People who do not trust God do stupid things.

Why was it stupid for David to go to Gath?

Tell how David went to Gath (Goliath's hometown) and acted insane to escape.

Day 5
Nob is destroyed (I Sam 22:1-23)

The purpose of today's lesson: Show how people are hurt when they help the man who is not trusting God.

Why did Saul destroy Nob?

Tell this story showing that Nob was destroyed for helping David and that David should have known better than getting them involved.

XI.   Week 11 Saul Pursue David (I Sam 23 – 26)

Day 1
David takes Keilah (I Sam 23:1-13)

The purpose of today's lesson: David continues to serve Israel.

Why did David strike Keilah despite the problem with Saul?

Tell how David took this city even though Saul was against him.

Day 2
Saul tries to trap David (I Sam 23:14-29)

The purpose of today's lesson: The jealous and bitter never rest or forgive.

Why didn't Saul recognize David's act of service?

Tell how Saul continued to pursue David despite all David did.

Day 3
David cuts off Saul's robe (I Sam 24:1-22)

The purpose of today's lesson: The man of God does not take vengeance.

Why didn't David kill Saul when he had the chance?

Tell how David could have killed Saul but didn't and why.

Day 4
Abigail (I Sam 25:1-44)

The purpose of today's lesson: Learn the wisdom of a Godly woman.

Why were Abigail's actions good?

Tell this story showing how Abigail was wiser than her husband was and helped Nabal despite his foolishness.

Day 5
David's second chance to kill Saul (I Sam 26:1-25)

The purpose of today's lesson: David was faithful to leave the judgement to God.

Why didn't David kill Saul this second time? Wasn't God giving him the chance?

Tell this story highlighting that David was true to leave judgement to God.

XII. Week 12 The End of the First King (I Sam 27 – 31)

Day 1
David returns to Gath (I Sam 27:1-12)

The purpose of today's lesson: When our friends leave us we first shelter with our enemies.

Why did David go to Gath again?

Explain how this was the only place David could hide without hurting others.

Day 2
Saul consults a medium (I Sam 28:1-25)

The purpose of today's lesson: Bitterness destroys our walk with God.

What is wrong with what Saul did?

Explain how Saul went to a witch to contact Samuel and how this was the worst thing he could do in the sight of God.

Day 3
David is sent away (I Sam 29:1-11)

The purpose of today's lesson: Our enemies will never trust us.

Why did they send David home?

Tell this story stressing that the Philistines would never trust David.

Day 4
Ziklag (I Sam 30:1-31)

The purpose of today's lesson: God helps us retrieve our losses.

Did David get his wives back?

Tell how David was able to get his wives back from the Amalekites and shared the spoil with all.

Day 5
Saul is destroyed (I Sam 31:1-13)

The purpose of today's lesson: Bitterness and jealousy will destroy you and your house.

What was the ultimate end of Saul?

Explain how Saul died and how his sin destroyed him and his family.

II Samuel

I. Week 1 Civil War (II Samuel 1, 2)

Day 1 David hears of Saul's death (II Sam 1:1-16)

The purpose of today's lesson: We are to take no pleasure in the death of God's fallen man.

Why was David happy that Saul was gone?

Explain that David did not rejoice in Saul's death because Saul's life was a tragedy of a man who did not follow God.

Day 2 David mourns the death of Jonathan and Saul (II Sam 1:17-27)

The purpose of today's lesson: People mourn the death of God's man.

Why did they mourn when Saul was not a good person?

Again explain that people are not to delight in the pain of others

Day 3 Two are made king (II Sam 2:1-11)

The purpose of today's lesson: Resistance to God's ways may continue every when things change.

Why wasn't David made king once Saul died?

Show that even when obstructions were removed David's way was blocked.

Day 4 Civil War (II Sam 2:12-17)

The purpose of today's lesson: War can be a part of God's purposes.

Who were on the two sides in this battle?

Explain that was is sometimes necessary.

Day 5 There is no vengence (II Sam 2:18-32)

The purpose of today's lesson: Battle is for God's purpose not men

Why did Joab seek revenge?

Explain that once victory was accomplished the battle was over.

II. Week 2 David Becomes King (II Sam 3-5)

Day 1 The war continues (II Sam 3:1-25)

The purpose of today's lesson: David flourished because he was God's man.

Why was David successful?

Explain that David was winning because he followed God.

Day 2 Abner is killed (II Sam 3:26-39)

The purpose of today's lesson: Do not go against men for your own gain.

Why didn't David kill Abner?

Explain that David understood that Abner was one of God's people and would not strike him.

Day 3 Ishbosheth is killed (II Sam 4:1-12)

The purpose of today's lesson: For the third time David defends the honor of his enemies.

What happened to the killers of Ishbosheth?

Explain why David executed the men who killed Ishbosheth.

Day 4 David is king over all Israel (II Sam 5:1-16)

The purpose of today's lesson: Once the obstacles are removed David is rewarded.

How long did it take David to become king from the time of his annointing?

Show God's ways are sure if not slow in man's eyes.

Day 5 War with the Philistines (II Sam 5:17-25)

<u>The purpose of today's lesson</u>: It is best to seek God first.

What did David do before each battle?

Show that David prayed first and God gave him the victory.

III.   Week 3 David's Kingdom is Established (II Sam 6, 7)

Day 1
Uzzah dies (II Sam 6:1-11)

<u>The purpose of today's lesson</u>: To emphasize the holiness of God.

Why did Uzzah die?

Tell this story reviewing how the ark was supposed to be moved and that Uzzah died because he was irreverent to God (vs. 7).

Day 2
David dances (II Sam 6:12-23)

<u>The purpose of today's lesson</u>: To show the difference in one who knows God and one who doesn't.

Why did David dance and why didn't Michal like it?

Tell this story showing that David knew God and rejoiced and Michal didn't know God and didn't understand.

Day 3
David dreams of a temple (II Sam 7:1-7)

<u>The purpose of today's lesson</u>: God chooses His own place.

Why didn't want a house of cedar?

Review this story showing that David was presumptuous thinking he knew what God wanted.

Day 4
God's covenant with David (II Sam 7:8-17)

The purpose of today's lesson: God establishes what He will do.

According to God's covenant, who will build God a house?

Tell the vision of Nathan showing that when God said no to David He promised David that Solomon would build the temple.

Day 5
David's prayer (II Sam 7:18-29)

The purpose of today's lesson: The proper response to God is humble acceptance of His plans.

How did David respond to God's revealed will?

Tell of David's prayer showing that he accepted what God wanted with humility.

IV. Week 4 David Wins at War (II Sam 8 – 11)

Day 1
Early Victory (II Sam 8)

The purpose of today's lesson: God blessed His man in all things.

Why was David successful?

Tell the story of this chapter showing that David won because God was with him.

Day 2
Kindness to Mephibosheth (II Sam 9)

The purpose of today's lesson: We are to keep our oaths.

Why did David care for Mephibosheth?

Tell this story showing that David blessed this man in fulfillment of his covenant to Jonathan.

Day 3
More victory (II Sam 10)

The purpose of today's lesson: When God is for you, you can't lose.

How did David keep on winning?

Show that David never lost because of his walk with God.

Day 4
David's first sin (II Sam 11:1-5)

The purpose of today's lesson: When we are in a good place we can become complacent.

Why did David sin with Bathsheba?

Tell this part of the story emphasizing that in his success David got lazy in his relationship with God.

Day 5
Uriah's death (II Sam 11:6-27)

The purpose of today's lesson: Hidden sin leads to more and worse sin.

Why did David ultimately have to kill Uriah?

Show that when David's attempts at a cover-up (lying) failed he had to resort to murder.

V. Week 5 Sin in the House (II Sam 12 – 13)

Day 1
Confronted by Nathan (II Sam 12:1-15)

The purpose of today's lesson: Be sure that your sin will find you.

How did everyone find out about David's treachery?

Tell the story of Nathan going before David in courage and revealing his sin.

Day 2
The child dies (II Sam 12:16-23)

The purpose of today's lesson: Accept God's judgement when you deserve it.

Why wasn't David upset when the child died?

Tell how David knew once the child had died that God had judged.

Day 3
Solomon is born (II Sam 12:24-31)

The purpose of today's lesson: Mercy comes many times in the midst of judgement.

Who was Solomon's mother?

Show that the next child born of Bathsheba was the child of promise.

Day 4
Amnon defiles Tamar (II Sam 13:1-23)

The purpose of today's lesson: Once sin enters the house the children suffer.

Why did Amnon think he could do this to his sister?

Tell this story showing that Amnon thought he could get away with this because of the sin of David.

Day 5
Absalom avenges Tamar (II Sam 13:24-39)

The purpose of today's lesson: When the father does not act problems multiply.

Why did Absalom kill Amnon?

Show that when David as king did nothing to judge the sin of Amnon Absalom took action.

VI. Week 6 The Rebellion of Absalom (II Sam 14 – 15)

Day 1
The woman of Tekoa (II Sam 14:1-20)

The purpose of today's lesson: God uses people who are trying to deceive.

What was the purpose of the woman of Tekoa?

Joab used treachery but God used it for good (Tell this story)

Day 2 (II Sam 14:21-33)
Absalom returns

The purpose of today's lesson: The love of a father is stronger than the love of a son.

Why did David allow Absalom to return?

Tell the story of Absalom's return, showing that David loved Absalom more than Absalom loved David.

Day 3
Absalom takes the kingdom (II Sam 15:1-12)

The purpose of today's lesson: Flattery can used to gain control.

How did Absalom win the heart of the people?

Tell this story showing that Absalom used flattery to win the hearts of the people.

Day 4 & 5
David flees (II Sam 15:13-37)

The purpose of today's lesson: If we neglect our duties the results can be devastating.

Why did David have to flee?

Tell the story of David's flight from Jerusalem emphasizing that he had to leave because he did not follow God's will.

VII. Week 7 The Kingdom in Turmoil (II Sam 16 – 17)

Day 1
Ziba (II Sam 16:1-4)

The purpose of today's lesson: When one is in distress his judgement in clouded.

Should David have seen through Ziba's lies?

Tell how Ziba fooled David.

Day 2
David is cursed (II Sam 16:5-14)

The purpose of today's lesson: Do not judge those who bring God's word.

Why didn't David judge the man who cursed him?

Tell this story in showing that David knew he was out of God's will and knew that the man may have brought God's word.

Day 3
Absalom enters Jerusalem (II Sam 16:15-23)

The purpose of today's lesson: God provides opportunities for His redemption.

Why was Hushai in the house?

Show that God provides for His redemption even in the midst of His man's defeat.

Day 4
Hushai's counsel (II Sam 17:1-14)

The purpose of today's lesson: Again God uses deception to accomplish His will.

Why did Hushai lie to Absalom?

Tell the story, emphasizing that Hushai lied to Absalom in accordance with God's will.

Day 5
Hushai saves David (II Sam 17:15-29)

The purpose of today's lesson: Now we see that God intended to bring down Absalom and restored David.

Why did God allow Hushai to lie?

The show that God uses Hushai's deception to save David.

VIII. Week 8 Civil War (II Sam 18, 19)

Day 1
Absalom dies (II Sam 18:1-18)

The purpose of today's lesson: Rebellion comes to a harsh end

How did Absalom die?

Tell about Absalom's death emphasizes the consequences of rebellion

Day 2
David mourns (II Sam 18:19-33)

The purpose of today's lesson: Neglect in a father turns to grief

Why did Absalom die and why was David sad?

Tell this story showing that Absalom's downfall was a result of David's neglect as a father and David suffered for it.

Day 3
Joab rebukes David (II Sam 19:1-8)

The purpose of today's lesson: Remember the people who make sacrifices for you

Why was Joab angry?

Tell this story showing that David needed to show gratitude to his people.

Day 4
David is restored (II Sam 19:9-45)

The purpose of today's lesson: God restores His choice even when they go astray

Did David return as king?

Show that even with his mistakes David was returned as king.

Day 5
Mephibosheth and Shimei (II Sam 19:9-45)

The purpose of today's lesson: God does not want us to forget our state and our commitments.

Why did David treat Shimei and Mephibosheth so well?

Show that David didn't judge Shimei and continued to love Mephibosheth.

Week 9 David's Kingdom (II Sam 20-22)

Day 1
The Second Rebellion (II Sam 20:1-12)

The purpose of today's lesson: Rebellion encourages more rebellion.

What would make Sheba think to go against David?

Show that one rebellion against authority encourages others.

Day 2
The Revolt is Ended (II Sam 20:13-26)

The purpose of today's lesson: The end of the rebel is always severe.

What happened to Sheba?

Demonstrate that rebels live a hard life and wise is the one who gets rid of them.

Day 3
Gibeon (II Sam 21:1-14)

The purpose of today's lesson: Promises are never forgotten.

Why was there a famine in Israel at this time?

Indicate that God expects His people to keep their word.

Day 4
War with the Philistines (II Sam 21:15-22)

The purpose of today's lesson: David's enemies never departed.

Why was war always a part of David's life?

Show that God said war would always be present and it was.

95

Day 5
The Song of Deliverance (II Sam 22)

The purpose of today's lesson: We must always recognize God's work in our life.

What was the focus of David's psalm?

Notice that he praised God for deliverance and didn't complain about the lack of peace.

Week 10 The Last Days (II Sam 23, 24)

Day 1
The Last Psalm (II Sam 23:1-7)

The purpose of today's lesson: From the beginning to the end, remember the Lord.

What was the theme of this last psalm?

Indicate that David always knew God's preeminence in David's life.

Day 2
The Mighty Men (II Sam 23:8-39)

The purpose of today's lesson: God raises up a mighty company to do His work.

Why were the mighty men part of David's kingdom?

Demonstrate that God always has men to do His work.

Day 3
The Census is Taken (II Sam 24:1-11)

The purpose of today's lesson: Lack of faith is always wrong.

Why was it wrong to count the fighting men?

Show that the census revealed David's trust in numbers and not in God.

Day 4
Judgement (II Sam 24:12-17)

I Chronicles

Note: The first 9 chapters of the first book of Chronicles is a review of genealogy. While I would never discount the importance of any aspect of scripture, I do not feel a detailed study of these chapters will be rewarding for our children. If you as the parents wish to review this section with your children, this will cause no difficulty in the operation of our class.

I. Week 1 David Becomes King (I Chron 10 - 12)

Day 1
Saul's family dies (I Chron 10)

The purpose of today's lesson: The disobedient suffer consequences

Why did Saul and hid family die at the hands of the Philistines?

Tell the story of chapter 10 emphasizing verse 13.

Day 2
David is anointed (I Chron 11:1 - 3)

The purpose of today's lesson: God's man is recognized.

Why was David anointed?

Remind your children that David was chosen by God long before this anointing.

Day 3
Jerusalem is conquered (I Chron 11:4 - 9)

The purpose of today's lesson: Jerusalem has been special for thousands of years.

What was the first place David conquered as king?

Tell of the conquest of Jerusalem reminding the children that Jerusalem has always been special.

Day 4
David's drink (I Chron 11:10 - 47)

The purpose of today's lesson: Faithful men make big sacrifices.

What did this story about the drink tell you about David's men?

Tell the story of the drink showing these men's bravery and faithfulness and how David recognized those qualities.

Day 5
The Mighty Men (I Chron 12)

The purpose of today's lesson: See the many great exploits of Godly men.

What do you think about these men?

Review the exploits of these men showing that they were blessed by God.

II. Week 2 (I Chron 13 - 15)

Day 1
The Ark (I Chron 13)

The purpose of today's lesson: God does not change His ways for anyone.

Why did David fear the Ark?

Review this story showing that David did not understand why God killed Uzza.

Day 2
David is blessed (I Chron 14:1 - 7)

The purpose of today's lesson: Children are a sign of God's prosperity.

From reading this how do you know that God has blessed David?

Read this section emphasizing the listing of the children as part of God's blessing.

Day 3
David defeats the Philistines (I Chron 14:8 - 17)

The purpose of today's lesson: To succeed always seek God's way.

Why did David win both battles?

Describes these two battles showing that David sought God first, obeyed God and was given the victory.

Day 4
David moves the Ark (I Chron 15:1 - 24)

The purpose of today's lesson: Men of God learn from their mistakes.

What did David learn from the death of Uzza?

Show that David learned from his mistake and had the Ark carried.

Day 5
David rejoices over the Ark (I Chron 15:25 - 29)

The purpose of today's lesson: When we meet with God all modesty is lost.

Why was it unusual for David to show his excitement?

Tell this story showing that as king David would not do what he did.

III. Week 3 David Establishes Worship (I Chron 16 - 17)

Day 1
A tent for the Ark (I Chron 16:1 - 7)

The purpose of today's lesson: The worship of God must be established.

Why did David set up a tent for the Ark?

Tell this story emphasizing the importance of the worship of God.

Day 2
Praise of thanksgiving (I Chron 16:8 - 36)

The purpose of today's lesson: We must always recognize God as the source of all blessings

What was the central message of the psalm?

Explain that we must always recognize God as the source of all good things.

Day 3
Worship before the Ark (I Chron 16:37 - 43)

The purpose of today's lesson: Specific provision for worship was instituted.

Why were these specific provisions given?

Discuss this section showing that worship was very important in this nation.

Day 4
God's covenant with David (I Chron 17:1 - 15)

The purpose of today's lesson: God tells His people His plans

Who would build the temple for God?

Discuss this covenant in regard to David and Solomon.

Day 5
David's prayerful response to God (I Chron 17:16 - 27)

The purpose of today's lesson: Men of God accept God's plan.

What was David's response to God's revelation?

Discuss David's response despite his personal disappointment.

IV. Week 4 David Walks with God (I Chron 18 - 21:17)

Day 1
David reinforces his kingdom (I Chron 18)

The purpose of today's lesson: God's blessing is complete.

Who is responsible for David's success?

Review this chapter showing that God blesses David in all areas.

Day 2
David's men are shamed (I Chron 19:1 - 9)

The purpose of today's lesson: Young men can act foolishly.

Why were David's men shamed?

Discuss this story showing the foolishness of this act.

Day 3
David defeats Ammon (I Chron 19:10 - 19)

The purpose of today's lesson: Men pay dearly for foolishness.

What happened to Ammon?

Explain how these men picked a fight and suffered greatly.

Day 4
David defeats the giants of Gath (I Chron 20)

The purpose of today's lesson: God brings victory against the odds.

Describe the men of Gath?

Tell the story showing that God brings victory against giants.

Day 5
David counts his men (I Chron 21:1 - 17)

The purpose of today's lesson: Disobedience can come at any time.

Why did God punish Israel?

Tell the census story showing that disobedience can come in prosperity and God will punish it.

Week 5 The Service of the Lord (I Chron 21 - 24)

Day 1
The Altar (I Chron 21:18 - 30)

The purpose of today's lesson: Gifts to God cost us something.

Why wouldn't David accept the altar for free?

Show that David knew that real gifts to God cost us.

Day 2
David prepares for the temple (I Chron 22:1 - 6)

The purpose of today's lesson: Men of God are asked to start works they will not see the end of.

Why was David's act a sign of his greatness?

Tell how David prepared the way for Solomon.

Day 3
Solomon takes the task to build the temple (I Chron 22:6 - 19)

The purpose of today's lesson: Many of the great works of God are done through the generations.

Who wanted to build the house of the Lord and eventually did?

Discuss the building of the temple emphasizing how David prepared the way but Solomon actually did the work relating this to our own experience in salvation of the lost and many other works of the church.

Day 4
New duties for the Levites (I Chron 23:1 - 32)

The purpose of today's lesson: God always reserves people to His service.

What were the duties of the Levites?

Discuss this chapter centering in on how God reserves people to do His work.

Day 5
The Levites (I Chron 24:1 - 31)

The purpose of today's lesson: God cares about the details of His ministers.

Why do we have so mush detail regarding the Levites?

Discuss this chapter with the last showing how much God cares about the people assigned to His ministry.

VI. Week 6 The Final Acts of David (I Chron 25 - 29)

Day 1
The Musicians (I Chron 25: 1 - 31)

The purpose of today's lesson: God continues to divide the responsibilities in His house.

What were the duties of the musicians?

Continue to tell how God puts together His people with specific duties to fulfill.

Day 2
The Gatekeepers (I Chron 26:1 - 32)

The purpose of today's lesson: God cares about every job regardless of the significance we place on it.

What do the gatekeepers do?

God cares as much about what the gatekeepers do as what the king does.

Day 3
The commanders of the army (I Chron 27:1 - 34)

The purpose of today's lesson: The military was also important in this day and place.

What does God think about the military?

The military was also important to God when it was a necessary part of life.

Day 4
David speaks about the temple (I Chron 28:1 - 21)

The purpose of today's lesson: **David reaffirms God's work through the generations**

Why did David think he did not build the temple?

Tell this story showing that men of God understand that God weaves the work of many men through the generations to achieve His purpose.

Day 5
The Offerings (I Chron 29:1 - 30)

The purpose of today's lesson: **God's people give willingly to God's work.**

What was the attitude of Israel when they gave to the temple?

Show that people who follow God will always give willingly to God's work and to see God's purposes accomplished.

I Kings

I. Week 1 Solomon Assumes the Throne (I Kings 1, 2)

Day 1
David grows old (I Kings 1:1-10)

The purpose of today's lesson: God cares for us in our old age.

Did David remain king to his old age?

Tell of David's last days especially how God cared for him.

Day 2
Bathsheba insures Solomon is made king (I Kings 1:11-37)

The purpose of today's lesson: God uses many methods to gain His purpose.

How does God insure that Solomon becomes king?

Tell this story showing that God used Bathsheba to insure Solomon would be king.

Day 3
Solomon anointed king (I Kings 1:38-53)

The purpose of today's lesson: God foils the plans of the wicked.

Why were Adonijah and Joab surprised?

Tell how Solomon's anointing caught these men by surprise.

Day 4
David gives Solomon his charge (I Kings 2:1-18)

The purpose of today's lesson: Fathers can pass vision to their sons.

What was the purpose of David's charge?

Tell the story of David's charge showing that fathers can give sons a great calling.

Day 5
Enemies are executed (I Kings 2:19-46)

The purpose of today's lesson: The untimely end of the enemies of God.

Why were Adonijah, Joab and Shimei killed?

Tell of the deaths with the moral being the consequences of going against God's purposes.

II. Week 2 Solomon's Early Reign (I Kings 3 - 5, II Chron 1 & 2)

Day 1
Solomon's wise choice (I Kings 3:1-15)

The purpose of today's lesson: One or two crucial choices can build a life.

Why did Solomon ask for wisdom?

Discuss Solomon's visit with God emphasizing his crucial right choice.

Day 2
Example of Solomon's wisdom (I Kings 3:16-28)

The purpose of today's lesson: Benefits of right choices can be seen immediately.

Why did the woman give up her own son?

Discuss this example of Solomon's wise judgments?

Day 3
Solomon's greatness (I Kings 4, II Chron 1)

The purpose of today's lesson: God can give His people magnificent prosperity.

Why was Solomon so prosperous?

Discuss Solomon's material goods showing it was part of God's blessing.

Day 4
Alliance with King Hiram (I Kings 5:1-12)

The purpose of today's lesson: God uses the ungodly to accomplish His will.

Why did Solomon make an alliance with Hiram?

Discuss this treaty showing that God used it to build the temple.

Day 5
Solomon recruits laborers (I Kings 5:13-18, II Chron 2)

The purpose of today's lesson: Even improper means can turn to doing God's will.

How did Solomon get labor to build the temple?

Show that slavery, which was bad, can end up doing God's purposes.

III. Week 3 Solomon Builds the Temple (I Kings 6 - 8, II Chron 3 - 7)

Day 1
Building the temple (I Kings 6, II Chron 3)

The purpose of today's lesson: Each man does his job.

What was God's main job for Solomon?

Tell how Solomon proceeded to do what God wanted.

Day 2
Solomon's palace (I Kings 7:1-12)

The purpose of today's lesson: God allows riches to those who follow Him.

Does God allow His men to succeed?

Show that Solomon had personal success while he walked with God.

Day 3
Hiram's contribution to the temple (I Kings 7:13-51)

The purpose of today's lesson: God allows others to make major contributions to His plans.

Why was Hiram part of building the temple?

Tell of Hiram's contribution showing that God uses many people.

Day 4
The Ark is brought to the temple (I Kings 8:1-11, II Chron 4, 5)

The purpose of today's lesson: God's presence abides in His plans.

What is the significance of the ark coming to the temple?

Show how bringing the ark signifies God's presence in His work.

Day 5
Solomon dedicates the temple (I Kings 8:12-66, II Chron 6, 7)

The purpose of today's lesson: Men of God have to set apart the things of God for the people.

What is the reason for the dedication?

Tell of the dedication, prayer and offering showing that these acts sanctified the temple in the hearts of the people.

IV. Week 4 Solomon's Downfall (I Kings 9 - 11, II Chron 8, 9)

Day 1
God warns Solomon (I Kings 9:1-9, II Chron 8)

The purpose of today's lesson: No matter how good things are we must follow God.

Why did God warn Solomon?

Tell this story showing that people are most vulnerable when things are good.

Day 2
Hiram's reward (I Kings 9:10-28)

The purpose of today's lesson: Contributors to God's plan frequently get a reward.

Why did Hiram get a reward?

Show why Hiram got a reward both in a worldly and a spiritual sense

Day 3
The Queen of Sheba (I Kings 10:1-13, II Chron 9:1-12)

The purpose of today's lesson: Men of God many times are famous.

What was the reason for Solomon's fame?

Show that Godly men can be both rich and famous.

Day 4
Solomon's incredible wealth (I Kings 10:14-29, II Chron 9:13-31)

The purpose of today's lesson: Great prosperity can lead to great vulnerability.

What was the reason for Solomon's vulnerability?

Retell of Solomon's great wealth showing that it made him vulnerable to sin.

Day 5
Solomon turns from God (I Kings 11)

The purpose of today's lesson: Many times at the height of success the man of God falls.

What is the lesson of Solomon's fall?

Tell of Solomon's fall accenting when life is good we need to be on guard.

V. Week 5 The Kingdom Divides (I Kings 12, 13, II Chron 10 - 11)

Day 1
Rehoboam acts foolishly (I Kings 12:1-15, II Chron 10)

The purpose of today's lesson: Be careful whose advice you take.

What caused the split of Israel?

Discuss how Rehoboam took bad advice and the consequences were terrible.

Day 2
The kingdom splits (I Kings 12:16-24, II Chron 11)

The purpose of today's lesson: The consequences of bad choices are very bad.

Why were people not dedicated to Rehoboam?

Show that a lack of commitment to Rehoboam led to the split.

Day 3
Jeroboam practices idolatry (I Kings 12:25-33)

The purpose of today's lesson: People turn from God when given a chance.

What did Jeroboam do wrong?

Discuss the sin of Jeroboam explaining how people turn from God when given a chance and showing this will have horrible consequences.

Day 4
Jeroboam warned (I Kings 13:1-10)

The purpose of today's lesson: God graciously warns before He punishes.

Why did God issue a warning?

Explain that even when we should know better God gives us a chance to repent.

Day 5
A prophet disobeys (I Kings 13:11-34)

The purpose of today's lesson: Men of God must follow the instructions of God.

What led the prophet to go ahead and eat?

Explain how this prophet was led to disobey by someone else.

VI. Week 6 Decay of God's People (I Kings 14 - 16, II Chron 12 - 17)

Day 1
Judgment against Jeroboam (I Kings 14:1-20)

The purpose of today's lesson: God will not allow idolatry.

What was Jeroboam's worse sin?

Tell how Jeroboam was judged for idolatry.

Day 2
Rehoboam leads Judah astray (I Kings 14:21-31, II Chron 12, 13)

The purpose of today's lesson: Idolatry destroys the whole kingdom.

Why did Rehoboam lie to the people?

Tell of Rehoboam's deception.

Day 3
Asa (I Kings 15:1-22, II Chron 14 - 16)

The purpose of today's lesson: Even in bad times good people come along.

How was Asa described?

Discuss the reign of Asa telling how he was good but neglected to destroy the idolatry.

Day 4
Jehosephat (I Kings 15:23-34, II Chron 17)

The purpose of today's lesson: Conflict develops based on devotion to God.

What was the result of conflict between Judah and Israel?

Tell how Judah and Israel fought because one followed God and the other didn't.

Day 5
Israel continues to walk away from God (I Kings 16)

The purpose of today's lesson: Once people reject God and take up false gods the results are disastrous.

Were there any good kings in Israel?

Discuss the chapter showing there were no good kings in Israel and they all sinned after the sin of Jeroboam (idolatry).

VII. Elijah (I Kings 17 - 19)

Day 1
Elijah predicts drought (I Kings 17:1-16)

The purpose of today's lesson: In the midst of disaster God raises up a deliverer.

What was God's reason for sending Elijah?

Elijah showed that God did not give up on Israel.

Day 2
Elijah raises the widow's son (I Kings 17:17-24)

The purpose of today's lesson: Working with God's purposes has its benefits.

Why did Elijah raise the son?

Show that this episode revealed God's blessing on people who walk in His purposes.

Day 3
Elijah meets Obediah (I Kings 18:1-19)

The purpose of today's lesson: God uses many people together.

What is Obediah's purpose?

God brings many men together to work together.

Day 4
Choose this day who you will serve (I Kings 18:20-35)

The purpose of today's lesson: God will bring everyone to a choice.

Why did God bring these people to a choice?

Tell this very popular story showing that God bring people to a choice.

Day 5
Elijah's prayer (I Kings 18:36-46)

The purpose of today's lesson: Men of God make sure that God gets the glory.

What was Elijah's response to God's work?

Show that Elijah gave the glory to God.

VIII. Ahab and Jezebel (I Kings 20 - 22, II Chron 18)

Day 1
Elijah flees from Jezebel (I Kings 19)

The purpose of today's lesson: Men fail to act in faith in even when they see God work.

What did Elijah do in response to the threat of Jezebel?

Tell this story of Elijah's lack of faith and God's provision.

Day 2
War with Aram (I Kings 20:1-25)

The purpose of today's lesson: Disobedient men of God are better than pagans in God's eyes.

Why did God let Ahab win?

Discuss how God favors His people even when they are sinners.

Day 3
A second war (I Kings 20:26-43)

The purpose of today's lesson: More victories of God's people even in their sorry state.

Why did Ahab keep winning?

Despite Ahab's evil God watched over him.

Day 4
Ahab steals Naboth's vineyard (I Kings 21)

The purpose of today's lesson: There is no limit to the evil of men.

What does this sin of Ahab tell you about men?

Ahab had everything but he coveted and took what he couldn't have.

Day 5
Ahab dies (I Kings 22, II Chron 18)

The purpose of today's lesson: Evil catches up with men who walk in it.

How did Ahab and Jezebel die?

Tell of the death of Ahab and Jezebel.

PROVERBS - God's Wisdom in Human Hands

I.   Week 1 The Sluggard

Day 1
A Little Sleep (Prov 6:6-11, 24:30-34, 26:14)

The purpose of today's lesson: To see the main sign of laziness.

Describe the basic sign of laziness.

Using these scriptures show what to look for in lazy people.

Day 2
Cannot Do Anything (Prov 13:24, 19:24, 21:25, 26:15)

The purpose of today's lesson: See that lazy people are absurd.

What is so silly about these lazy people?

Show that lazy people are absurd in their inability to do things.

Day 3
There's a Lion in the Street (Prov 22:13, 26:13)

The purpose of today's lesson: Understand the excuses of the lazy are ridiculous.

How silly is this excuse?

Explain how silly the excuses of the lazy are.

Day 4
Rewards of the Sluggard (Prov 13:4, 15:19, 20:4, 21:25)

The purpose of today's lesson: Demonstrate that laziness leads to destruction.

What happens to the lazy person?

Using these and prior scriptures show that laziness leads to devastation.

Day 5
The Friends of a Sluggard (Prov 10:26)

The purpose of today's lesson: People who know lazy people get tired of them.

How does the friend of the lazy person free about that person?

Show that the friend of the lazy person is hurt by his laziness.

II.   Week 2 The Tongue

Day 1
The Value of the Tongue Prov 25:11, 10:20, 12:18, 15:4

The purpose of today's lesson: To see the value of proper words

What value does God put on proper words

Use these scriptures to show God's feeling about good speech.

Day 2
Destruction and the Tongue Prov 6:17, 6:24, 26:28

The purpose of today's lesson: Show hoe destructive words can be.

Is the phrase, "Sticks and stones can break my bones but words cannot hurt me." correct?

Show that words cause more damage than we realize.

Day 3
The Power of the Tongue Prov 18:21, 25:15

The purpose of today's lesson: Demonstrate the tongue has great power.

How destructive or constructive are words?

Show that words can bring life and death.

Day 4
Reward and Punishment Prov 10:31, 21:23

The purpose of today's lesson: Show the results of good and bad speech.

What are the benefits and punishments for geed and bad words?

Discuss the rewards of good speech and punishment for bad speech.

Day 5
Good Advice Prov 17:27,28, 18:2

The purpose of today's lesson: Receive good advice regarding our speech.

Is it better to talk or stay quiet?

Discuss the value of silence.

III. Week 3 The Wise Man

Day 1
The Path of Wisdom Prov 2:1-22

The purpose of today's lesson: See that God has called us to a walk with wisdom.

What is one of the most important things we can have?

Discuss the path of wisdom God has provided.

Day 2
The Pursuit of Wisdom Prov 4:1-13

The purpose of today's lesson: See that wisdom is something to be pursued.

How does one gain wisdom?

Show that the acquisition of wisdom is a pursuit not sudden.

Day 3
A Father's Instruction Prov 6:20-24, 7:1-5

The purpose of today's lesson: Understand the value of a father's instruction.

Where does one gain much of their wisdom?

Demonstrate that a father is the primary source of wisdom.

Day 4
Incline Your Ear Prov 5:1-2, 22:17-21

The purpose of today's lesson: See the value of attentive listening.

What are the ways we get wisdom?

Show that hearing and listening are very important.

Day 5
Reward of Wisdom Prov 8:1-24

The purpose of today's lesson: Understand the rewards of obtaining wisdom.

What are some rewards of wisdom?

Show the many rewards of wisdom.

IV.   Week 4 The Fool (Part 1)

Day 1
The Way of a Fool (Prov 12:15; 17:12; 28:26)

The purpose of today's lesson: If you trust only yourself you are a fool.

How does one keep from bring foolish?

Show that one must trust God to keep from being a fool.

Day 2
Spreads Bad Words (Prov 10:18, 27:3)

The purpose of today's lesson: One who spreads discord is a fool.

What is a foolish thing to do?

Show that gossip and talking bad about others is foolish.

Day 3
Is Foolish (Prov 13:16; 14:16)

The purpose of today's lesson: A fool is easy to recognize.

How does a fool act?

Explain that a fool will always show themselves eventually.

Day 4
Undiscerning (Prov 14:7; 17:10; 23:9)

The purpose of today's lesson: One who cannot see what is right is a fool.

What is another sign of a fool?

Describe how a fool cannot decide what is best.

Day 5
Regrets a Father's Advice (Prov 15:5)

The purpose of today's lesson: Unlike a wise child the fool fails to listen to his father.

What is a difference between a wise and a foolish person?

Explain that one important difference between the wise and the foolish is listening to a father's instruction.

V. Week 5 The Fool (Part 2)

Day 1
Brings Misery to His Parents (Prov 17:21)

The purpose of today's lesson: A fool grieves his parents.

What effect does a fool have on his family?

Show that a fool brings grief and embarrassment to his family.

Day 2
Does Not Control His Speech (Prov 18:2; 19:1; 20:3; 29:20)

The purpose of today's lesson: The fool cannot speak properly.

What is a second important difference between the fool and the wise man?

Explain that the fool cannot control his speech unlike the wise man.

Day 3
Does Not Receive Prosperity (Prov 19:10)

The purpose of today's lesson: God reserves long term prosperity for the wise.

Who ultimately receives prosperity?

Show that the fool does not receive lasting prosperity.

Day 4
Cannot Receive Wisdom (Prov 24:7; 27:22)

The purpose of today's lesson: The fool is unable to receive wisdom.

Can the fool ever receive wisdom?

Show that a fool cannot consistently walk in wisdom.

Day 5
Undeserving of Honor (Prov 26:1,8)

The purpose of today's lesson: The fool deserves no recognition.

What is a fool's reward?

Describe how a fool gets no reward.

VI.   Week 6 Advice to Young People (Part 1)

Day 1
Key Remembrance (Prov 1:2-4)

The purpose of today's lesson: To know the key principles of life.

What are the key things to remember as a young person?

Explain the key principles to remember as one goes out on their own.

Day 2
Temptation in the World (Prov 1:10-19)

The purpose of today's lesson: Understand the world is full of temptations.

What will the world try to get you into?

Clarify the way the world is full of bad opportunities.

Day 3
The School of Wisdom (Prov 1:20-33)

The purpose of today's lesson: Find where the real college is.

Where is the best source of learning?

Describe that The Bible and God are the best places to learn.

Day 4
The Young Persons' Enemies (Prov 2:10-22)

The purpose of today's lesson: Recognize a young person's enemies.

What are a young person's enemies?

After reading these verses see if you can identify enemies of young people.

Day 5
Listen to God's Law (Prov 3:1-8)

The purpose of today's lesson: Appreciate the importance of staying in God's law.

What is one of the most vital things to do as a young person?

Explain the significance of continuing in God's Law.

VII. Week 7 Advice to Young People (Part 2)

Day 1
Chastening of the Lord (Prov 3:11-12)

The purpose of today's lesson: See that God's (and a parent's) correction is good.

How should we feel about our parents when we are punished?

Explain why correction is good (Also see Job 5:17-18).

Day 2
Remember a Father's Instruction (Prov 4:1-22)

The purpose of today's lesson: Learn where our anchors are in a confusing world.

How does one decide what is right and wrong?

Clarify that out in the world there are many opinions and ways of doing things. A father's instruction is how one measures these opinions.

Day 3
Strange Women (Prov 5:1-15; 7:6-27)

The purpose of today's lesson: Understand that God desires us to be pure in our actions.

What is God's design regarding purity?

Use these scriptures to discuss sexual purity with your child at whatever level you feel they are.

Day 4
Marriage (Prov 5:16-23)

The purpose of today's lesson: Discover God's plan for marriage.

What does God want for us in marriage?

Discuss marriage with your children.

Day 5
Seven Things God Hates (Prov 6:16-23)

The purpose of today's lesson: Find out some things God does not like.

What are seven things God hates?

Review these seven things discussing each one.

VIII. Nuggets for Life Sept 4

Day 1
The Heart (Prov 15:11-33)

The purpose of today's lesson: Realize the importance of the heart.

What does the Bible say about the heart?

Discuss the important of the heart.

Day 2
False Balance (Prov 11:1; 20:10)

The purpose of today's lesson: See what God thinks about dishonesty.

How does God feel about dishonesty?

Use this to talk to your child about honesty in business.

Day 3
Your Reputation (Prov 22:1; 19:1; 20:7)

The purpose of today's lesson: Realize the value of a good reputation.

What is more important money or a good reputation?

Contrast the value of a good name and money.

Day 4
Lying (Prov 12:22; 13:5; 14:25; 19:5)

The purpose of today's lesson: Appreciate the problem with telling lies.

What is the extent of trouble associated with lying?

Use these scriptures to go over the problem of lying.

Day 5
Joy is Good for the Soul (Prov 17:22)

The purpose of today's lesson: Recognize the value of a merry heart.

What is more valuable to the body than medicine?

Explain this scripture and the relationship between health and joy.

IX. Week 9 Relationships

Day 1
Source of Arguments (Prov 13:10)

The purpose of today's lesson: Learn the source of all arguments

What is the source of all contention?

Discuss the central nature of pride to all disagreements.

Day 2
Value of a Good Friend (Prov 17:17; 27:9-10; 27:17)

The purpose of today's lesson: Understand the value of true friends.

What are the rewards of having good friends?

Show your children the importance of good friends.

Day 3
The Rod (Prov 13:24; 22:15; 23:13)

The purpose of today's lesson: Find out the reason for spankings.

Why do parents spank children?

Illustrate that spanking is important in training.

Day 4
Your Neighbor (Prov 14:21)

The purpose of today's lesson: Learn that neighbors and our relationship to them is important.

What is the proper relationship to our neighbors?

Discuss this aspect of relationship.

Day 5
Be Friendly (Prov 18:24)

The purpose of today's lesson: Know our approach to relationships.

What should be our overriding attitude towards others?

Use this scripture to help children see that love and friendliness is our attitude toward others.

The Life of Jesus —Part 1

I. **Week 1 A Child is Born (Lk 1 - 2:20, 3:23-38, Mt 1:1 – 2:12, Jn 1:1-18)**

Day 1
The ancestry of Jesus (Mt 1:1-17, Luke 3:23-38)

The purpose of today's lesson: Understand the ancestry of Jesus

What is the purpose of these family trees?

Discuss both family trees explaining Jesus was a descendant of Abraham (the Jews) and Adam (all man kind).

Day 2 The Word became flesh (Jn 1:1-18)

The purpose of today's lesson: Know the theology of Jesus' life.

Why was Jesus described as the Word and Light?

Talk about this passage showing that John was telling us who Jesus really was.

Day 3
John is born (Lk 1:5-25, 57-80)

The purpose of today's lesson: See John as the forerunner of Jesus.

What was the purpose of the life of John the Baptist?

Talk about the birth of John showing him as the proclaimer of Jesus even in his birth.

Day 4
The promise of Jesus (Mt 1:18-25, Lk 1:26-56)

The purpose of today's lesson: A miraculous life proclaimed

Why did God tell us Jesus was coming?

Talk about this story emphasizing the need for God to proclaim Jesus' birth.

Day 5
Jesus is Born (Mt 2:1-12; Lk 2:1-20)

The purpose of today's lesson: To see the important parts of the day Jesus was born.

What were some things that made the birth of Jesus special? What was not special?

Tell this familiar story with an emphasis on the miraculous but also on humble beginnings.

II. Preparation for Ministry (Mt 2:13-4:11, Mk 1:1-13, Lk 2:21-3:22, 4:1-13, Jn 1:19-35)

Day 1
Anna and Simeon (Lk 2:25-40)

The purpose of today's lesson: To see how Jesus was the fulfillment of the Old Testament.

What was the promise to Simeon and Anna?

Tell this story showing that God had promised to show both Simeon and Anna the salvation of Israel.

Day 2
Jesus the boy (Mt 2:13-23, Lk 2:41-52)

The purpose of today's lesson: Relate Jesus as a boy to all children.

What was Jesus' life like as he grew up?

Tell this story showing that Jesus obeyed his parents and grew in favor with God and men.

Day 3
The Ministry of John the Baptist (Mt 3:1-12, Mk1:1-8, Lk 3:1-20, Jn 1:19-35)

The purpose of today's lesson: **Understand the purpose of John.**

What was God's purpose for John's life?

Discuss John the Baptist showing he had a specific calling which he fulfilled.

Day 4
The Baptism of Jesus (Mt 3:13-17, Mk 1:9-11, Lk 3:21-22)

The purpose of today's lesson: **Realize that baptism was a part of the man's preparation before God.**

Why was Jesus baptized?

Tell this story showing that all men of God are consecrated to God and that God is well pleased.

Day 5
The temptation of Jesus (Mt 4:1-11, Mk 1:12,13, Lk 4:1-13)

The purpose of today's lesson: **See Jesus went through everything we go through,**

Why was Jesus tempted?

Show that Jesus was tempted to understand our struggle and so we could see the importance of scripture in overcoming temptation.

III. **Week 3 Early Ministry I (Mt 4:12-17, Mk 1:14,15, Lk 3:19,20, 4:14,15, Jn 1:35-4:42)**

Day1
Early disciples, early miracles (Jn1:35 - 2:12)

The purpose of today's lesson: **God affirmed the ministry of Jesus.**

What did Jesus do early in His ministry?

Describe how early on God affirmed Jesus with the miraculous.

Day 2
Jesus clears the temple, John jailed (Jn 2:12-25, Lk 3:19,20)

Ths purpose of today's lesson: Jesus was not a man of the people, He was a man of GOD.

What was the problem in the temple?

Tell this story showing the corruption of the temple and Jesus' response.

Day 3
Born again (Jn 3:1-36)

The purpose of today's lesson: First notion of the essence of the Gospel.

What was the primary message of Jesus to Nicodemus?

Tell this story explaining the primary message of the Gospel.

Day 4
The Kingdom of Heaven is at hand (Mt 4:12-17, Mk 1:14,15, Lk 4:14,15)

The purpose of today's lesson: To see the early message of Jesus and the response.

What was the early message of Jesus and what was the response?

Use this to begin to explain the concept of the Kingdom of God.

Day 5
The Samaritan Woman (Jn 4:1-42)

The purpose of today's lesson: To see how Jesus shared the Gospel.

How did Jesus go about telling people about himself?

This familiar story gives the opportunity to demonstrate how Jesus shared about Himself and His Kingdom.

IV. Week 4 Early Ministry II (Mt 4:18-25, 8:1-9:13, Mk 1:16-2:17, 5:1-20, Lk 4:16-5:11, 8:26-40, Jn 4:43-54)

Day 1
Jesus casts out devils (Mt 8:28-34, Mk 5:1-20, Luke 8:26-40)

The purpose of today's lesson: To show the authority of Jesus.

Why did the demons have to listen to Jesus?

This story shows the authority of the man of God over the spirit realm.

Day 2
Jesus heals (Mt 8:1-17, 9:1-8, Mk 1:29-34, 1:40-2:1-12, Jn 4:43-54)

The purpose of today's lesson: To touch a person you must be concerned with all of him.

What did Jesus do during this time?

Discuss how Jesus not only touched the spirit but also the physical and why that was important.

Day 3
Fishers of men (Mt 4:18-22, Mk 1:16-20, Lk 4:16-30)

The purpose of today's lesson: Our call is to bring people to Jesus.

What does it mean to be a fisher of men?

Tell how Jesus called people to a higher purpose.

Day 4
Jesus' fame (Mt 4:23-25, 9:9-13, Mk 1:21-28, 35-39, 2:13-17, Lk 4:31-37, 42-44)

The purpose of today's lesson: Many times one is loved early on.

What did people think of Jesus early in His ministry?

Tell this story showing that Jesus had fame early because He touched the selfish part of man.

Day 5
Miracles establish word (Lk 5:1-11)

The purpose of today's lesson: God uses the miraculous to establish his Word.

What is the primary purpose of miracles?

Show that Jesus uses His miracles to establish His Word.

V. Week 5 Early Claims (Mt 9:14-17, 12:1-21, 5:1-16, Mk 2:18- 3:19, Lk 5:33-6:26, Jn 5)

Day1
The Son of God (Jn 5)

The purpose of today's lesson: We need to see Jesus as the Son of God.

In this story what did Jesus say about Himself?

Help the child understand the claim of son ship and why that was significant.

Day 2
The Bridegroom (Mt 9:14-17, Mk 2:18-22, Lk 5:33-39)

The purpose of today's lesson: We need to see Jesus as our bridegroom.

Why is Jesus the bridegroom?

Demonstrate the important of the fact that Jesus will be our bridegroom.

Day 3
Lord of the Sabbath (Mt 12:1-21, Mk 2:23-3:6, Lk 6:1-11)

The purpose of today's lesson: We need to see Jesus as the Lord of God's world.

Why could Jesus do what was unlawful in the Jews eyes?

Show that Jesus was not overthrowing the Law but had authority to expand on the Jews' interpretation of the Law.

Day 4
Great teacher (Mt 5:1-16, Lk 6:20-26)

The purpose of today's lesson: We need to see Jesus as a great teacher.

Is it important to study what Jesus taught?

Show that Jesus was profound in His teaching to the Jews and to us.

Day 5
Jesus chooses the twelve (Mk 3:13-19, Lk 6:12-19)

The purpose of today's lesson: We need to see Jesus as one who calls people to Himself.

How did one become close to Jesus?

People who know God are called to that place by God.

VI. Week 6 Be Not As They Are: Part 1 (Mt 5:17 - 6:18, Lk 6:27-36)

Day1
The law and anger (Mt 5:17-26)

The purpose of today's lesson: Anger (source of broken relationship) is equal to murder.

Why was anger so important?

Describe how anger as the source of broken relationship is as bad as murder.

Day 2
Lust and divorce (Mt 5:27-32)

The purpose of today's lesson: The heart is as important as our actions.

Where do our actions come from?

Tell how the heart makes us what we are and therefore must be guarded.

Day3
Vows and retaliation (Mt 5:33-42)

The purpose of today's lesson: Like God's Words our words are important.

Why is breaking our vows so important?

Show the high premium God puts on our words.

Day 4
Enemies and giving (Mt 5:43-6:4, Lk 6:27-36)

The purpose of today's lesson: God desires healing of broken relationships.

Why does God call us to love our enemies?

Discuss how God wants us to take steps to heal relationships.

Day 5
Prayer and fasting (Mt 6:5-18)

The purpose of today's lesson: Fasting is not a religious show

What is the true purpose of fasting?

Contrast the difference between a religious show and true devotion to God in fasting.

VII. Week 7 Be Not as They Are Part 2 (Mt 6:19-7:29, 11:1-19, Lk 6:37-49, 7:11-35)

Day 1
Trust One Master (Mt 6:19-34)

The purpose of today's lesson: Learn there is only one we can and must trust.

Who is the only one we can trust?

Illustrate that trusting God replaces fear and anxiety.

Day 2
Judging Others (Mt 7:1-23, Lk 6:37-42)

The purpose of today's lesson: Learn the proper and improper way to judge.

How should we go about judging things around us?

Show that there is an improper way to judge but that there is a proper way as well.

Day 3
A Tree is known by its Fruit (Lk 6:43-45)

The purpose of today's lesson: Understand how to discern.

How does one discern things or another person.

Demonstrate that what a life produces shows what is inside.

Day 4
Where is Your House Built? (Mt 7:24-29, Lk 6:46-49)

The purpose of today's lesson: Understand the importance of doing God's Word.

What should we do once God shows us something in the Bible?

Explain how we must do what God confirms in His Word.

Day 5
Raising the dead and talking to John (Mt 11:1-19, Lk 7:11-35)

The purpose of today's lesson: A man of God will see his purpose fulfilled.

Why was John interested in Jesus even in prison?

Discuss how John knew his purpose was fulfilled when Jesus came.

VIII. Teaching in Parables (Mt 11:20-13:30, Mk 3:31-4:34, 12:22-37, Lk 7:36-8:18)

Day1
Rest for the soul (Mt 11:20-30, Lk 7:36-50)

The purpose of today's lesson: Jesus promises rest for those who labored against the Law.

How does one get rest from the struggle of life?

Describe how God promises rest in Jesus from the weight of the Law.

Day 2
First accusation (Mt 12:22-37, Lk 8:1-3)

The purpose of today's lesson: Preaching the Kingdom will produce opposition.

What was the accusation against Jesus?

Tell how the Pharisees accused Jesus of being in league with the devil and Jesus' answer.

Day 3
The family of God (Mt 12:38-50, Mk 3:31-35, Lk 8:19-21)

The purpose of today's lesson: Relationship to God is defined spiritually not physically.

Why did Jesus say that the disciples were His family?

Show that Jesus defined His family in the spirit and not physically.

Day 4
Parable of the four soils (Mt 13:1-23, Mk 4:1-25, Lk 8:4-18)

The purpose of today's lesson: We need to receive God's Word the right way.

What are the ways the Word of God is received?

Go through this parable explaining the right and wrong way to receive God's Word.

Day 5
The Wheat and the Tares (Mt 13:24-30)

<u>**The purpose of today's lesson**</u>: **What we bring into our minds is important.**

What is the difference between the wheat and the tares?

The seed as the Word of God can be polluted by the philosophies of the world.

LIFE OF JESUS - 2

I. Week 1 Parables of Jesus (Mt 8:23-34, 9:18-34, 13:31-52; Mk 4:30-5:43; Lk 8:22-56)

Day 1
Parable of mustard seed & yeast (Mt 13:31-35;Mk 4:30-34)

The purpose of today's lesson: Understand these parables

What was Jesus trying to say in these parables?

Explain these parables to your children.

Day 2
Parable of weeds and hidden treasure (Mt 13:36-44)

The purpose of today's lesson: Learn about these parables

What was Jesus saying in these parables?

Explain these parables to your children.

Day 3
Parable of pearl and fishing net (Mt 13: 45-52)

The purpose of today's lesson: Review these parables

What was Jesus trying to teach in these parables?

Explain these parables to your children.

Day 4

Calming the storm and taming the demons (Mt 8:23-34; Mk 4:35-5:20; Lk 8:22-39)

The purpose of today's lesson: See the great power of Jesus

What did the demons say about Jesus?

Tell these stories emphasizing Jesus' great power as a man of faith.

Day 5
More healings (Mt 9:18-34; Mk 5:21-43; Lk 8:40-56)

The purpose of today's lesson: Understand that Jesus continued to heal

Why did Jesus continue to heal?

Tell this story showing the compassion of Jesus.

II. Week 2 The Ministry of Jesus (Mt 9:35-10:42, 13:53-14:36; Mk 6:1-56; Lk 9:1-17; Jn 6:1-59)

Day 1
Doubt and prayer (Mt 13:53-58, 9:35-38; Mk 6:1-6)

The purpose of today's lesson: Show that people must have faith.

Why was Jesus not able to heal?

Tell this story showing that even Jesus required the faith of the people.

Day 2
The work of the twelve (Mt 10:1-42; Mk 6:7-13; Lk 9:1-6)

The purpose of today's lesson: Understand how Jesus sent out his 12.

Why did Jesus warn the 12?

Talk about the 12 and what their problems were going to be.

Day 3
John killed and Jesus feeds the multitude (Mt 14:1-21; Mk 6:14-44; Lk 9:7-17; Jn 6:1-15)

<u>The purpose of today's lesson</u>: Know why John was killed.

Why did John have to die?

Tell this story explaining John's death and the feeding.

Day 4
Jesus walks on water and continues to heal (Mt 14:22-36; Mk 6:45-56; Jn 6:16-21)

<u>The purpose of today's lesson</u>: Know why we keep our eyes on Jesus.

Why did Peter walk on water and then sink?

Tell this story showing that Peter sank when his eyes went off Jesus.

Day 5
The bread of heaven (Jn 6: 22-59)

<u>The purpose of today's lesson</u>: Learn how Jesus sustains us.

What did Jesus mean when He called Himself the bread of heaven?

Explain what Jesus meant in this story.

LIFE OF JESUS - 2

III. Week 3 Continued Ministry (Mt 15:1-16:26; Mk 7:1-9:1; Lk 9:18-27; Jn 6:60-71)

Day 1
Jesus deserted (Jn 6:60-71; Mt 15:1-20; Mk 7:1-23)

The purpose of today's lesson: Many desert Jesus when faced with the truth of His life

Why did the disciples leave Jesus?

Talk about this story showing that following Jesus not always popular.

Day 2
Healing continues (Mt 15:21-31; Mk 7:24-37)

The purpose of today's lesson: Despite His fame Jesus continues to heal

Why did Jesus continue to heal?

Recount this statement showing Jesus' empathy.

Day 3
Jesus feeds four thousand (Mt 15:32-16:4; Mk 8:1-13)

The purpose of today's lesson: Jesus takes care of physical needs.

What was Jesus saying with this feeding?

Narrate this miracle discussing what Jesus was showing us.

Day 4
Jesus' warning (Mt 16:5-12; Mk 8:14-26)

The purpose of today's lesson: When Jesus warns, listen.

What was the main warning?

Discuss the importance of avoiding bad teaching.

Day 5
The Messiah (Mt 16:13-26; Mk 8:27-9:1; Lk 9:18-27)

The purpose of today's lesson: Most important revelation ever.

What is the single most important fact about Jesus?

Talk about Jesus as the Messiah.

IV. Week 4 Continued Ministry (Mt 17:1-18:35; Mk 9:2-50; Lk 9:28-50)

Day 1
Jesus transfigured (Mt 17:1-21; Mk 9:2-29; Lk 9:28-43)

The purpose of today's lesson: We see His true glory

What did we find out about Jesus in this story?

Tell how Jesus was shown in His true glory (only after the revelation).

Day 2
Jesus predicts His death (Mt 17:22-27; Mk 9:30-32)

The purpose of today's lesson: Jesus knew His death was coming.

Why did Jesus predict His death?

Discuss how Jesus' death will not be an accident.

Day 3
Disciples show weakness (Mt 18:1-6; Mk 9:33-41; Lk 9:44-50)

The purpose of today's lesson: **The followers of Jesus, like us, are real people.**

How do the disciples show they are real people?

Tell this story showing that the disciples are just like us.

Day 4
Jesus' warnings (Mt 18:7-14; Mk 9:42-50)

The purpose of today's lesson: **Be careful against spiritual pride**

What was Jesus warning against?

Explain these warnings from the perspective of spiritual pride.

Day 5
Dealing with sinners (Mt 18:15-35)

The purpose of today's lesson: **Learning proper behavior with fallen brothers**

How should one act with a brother who sins?

Explain the teaching of Jesus in this regard.

V. Week 5 Continued Ministry (Mt 8:18-22; Lk 9:51-10:16; Jn 7:1-8:59)

Day 1
Cost of Discipleship (Jn 7:1-9; Mt 8:18-22; Lk 9:51-62)

The purpose of today's lesson: See that following Jesus has a price.

What is the price for following Jesus?

Tell this story showing that following Jesus has a cost (Make sure to give examples from your experience.)

Day 2
Jesus Challenges Religious Leaders (Jn 7:10-52)

The purpose of today's lesson: Following Jesus is different from religion.

Why did Jesus fight with the Pharisees?

Explain that devotion to Jesus is different and sometimes in opposition to religion. (This is an extremely important concept in our culture. Spend whatever time it takes)

Day 3
Jesus Shows Us Compassion (Jn 7:53-8:20)

The purpose of today's lesson: Determine the Church is the source of grace.

What was Jesus' attitude toward sinners?

Reveal the importance of grace coming from the church while judgment comes from religion (another crucial lesson. Take time to give experiences of when grace was shown to you).

Day 4
God's True Children (Jn 8:21-59)

The purpose of today's lesson: Master what makes a person a true disciple.

What was the conflict between Jesus and the religious leaders?

This is another important lesson in our culture. Make sure your child understands the difference between religion and relationship with God.

Day 5
Jesus Sends Out Messengers (Lk 10:1-16)

The purpose of today's lesson: God will provide for His workers

Why did Jesus tell His men not to take from the people they visited?

Show that Jesus expects us to trust Him when we work for Him.

VI. Week 6 Continued Ministry (Lk 10:17-12:21)

Day 1
The Good Samaritan (Lk 10:17-37)

The purpose of today's lesson: Understand that works mean more than words or position.

Why didn't anyone else stop?

Tell how God is interested in our hearts and what we do.

Day 2
Teach Us to Pray (Lk 10:38-11:13)

The purpose of today's lesson: Jesus gave us road map to pray.

When did Jesus teach them about prayer?

Tell how Jesus instructed them (and us) about prayer.

Day 3
Jesus Confronts Hostility (Lk 11:14-32)

The purpose of today's lesson: We will have to confront persecution.

What was Jesus' response to persecution?

Teach your children about confrontation in love giving examples from you life if possible.

Day 4
The Light Within (Lk 11:33-54)

The purpose of today's lesson: Know where our spiritual life is and comes from.

What is the importance of the eye?

Teach your child that the eye is the gate to the soul.

Day 5
The Rich Fool (Lk 12:1-21)

The purpose of today's lesson: Learn nothing in life is guaranteed

Why was it foolish to build new barns?

Explain that in our culture we take our life for granted and God says this is foolish.

VII. Week 7 Continued Ministry (Lk 12:22-13:21; Jn 9:1-41)

Day 1
Worry Not (Lk 12:22-48)

The purpose of today's lesson: We must trust God

Why should we not worry?

Tell the story Jesus told explaining our need to trust God?

Day 2
Future Crisis (Lk 12:49-59)

The purpose of today's lesson: The lessons of Jesus will divide people.

Why did Jesus say this?

Teach that the truth of the Gospel will divide even families.

Day 3
Repent (Lk 13:1-17)

The purpose of today's lesson: All face judgment and must repent.

When Jesus was told of tragedy He was not moved. Why

Tell this story showing that repentance is more important than other considerations (Another very important lesson since in our culture people bring up other issues).

Day 4
Kingdom of God (Lk 13:18-21)

The purpose of today's lesson: Start learning about the Kingdom of God.

What is the Kingdom of God compared to?

Explain these two example of the Kingdom.

Day 5
Man Born Blind (Jn 9:1-41)

The purpose of today's lesson: The power of Jesus cannot be denied

Why were the Pharisees so upset about the healing?

Show that this healing reaffirmed Jesus' power and authority.

VIII. Week 8 Continued Ministry (Lk 13:22-15:10; Jn 10:1-42)

Day 1
The Good Shepherd (Jn 10:1-42)

The purpose of today's lesson: Jesus is there to lead us and protect us.

What is the importance of the image of a shepherd?

Explain why Jesus used the image of a shepherd.

Day 2
Grief Over Jerusalem (Lk 13:22-35)

The purpose of today's lesson: Jesus grieves over His people.

What was in Jesus' heart towards the Jews?

Tells this story explaining that God's heart is always compassion.

Day 3
Seeking Honor (Lk 14:1-14)

The purpose of today's lesson: **Never seek honor but accept it graciously**

Why should we always take the last place?

Show that we should never seek honor but when offered we can accept it.

Day 4
Cost of Discipleship (Lk 14:15-35)

The purpose of today's lesson: **Nothing is more important than the Kingdom of God.**

What should always have first priority in our lives?

Discuss how we should never let other concerns get in the way of the Kingdom of God and its priorities.

Day 5
Care for the Lost (Lk 15:1-10)

The purpose of today's lesson: **God will do anything to bring one to salvation.**

Why would Jesus commend leaving 99 to find one?

Use this story to emphasize the importance to God (and hopefully to us) of one lost soul.

LIFE OF JESUS - III

I. **Week 1 Parables and Ministry (Luke 15:8-18:14, Jn 11)**

Day 1
Lost and found (Luke 15:8-32)

<u>The purpose of today's lesson</u>: See the value Jesus places on the lost.

What was important to Jesus in the parable of the lost coin?

Show that saving the lost is more important than preserving souls.

Day 2
Lazarus in heaven (Luke 16-17:10)

<u>The purpose of today's lesson</u>: There is no relationship between this world's success and the Kingdom of God.

Why was Lazarus in heaven and the rich man not.

Explain that God has a special heart for those that suffer in this life.

Day 3
I am the resurrection (Jn 11)

<u>The purpose of today's lesson</u>: See that Jesus is the only way of resurrection.

Why did Jesus let Lazarus (different one) die?

Demonstrate how Jesus showed He was the only hope of resurrection.

Day 4
Healing lepers (Luke 17:11-37)

The purpose of today's lesson: We must always be thankful.

What was Jesus upset about with the lepers?

Illustrate our need to be grateful for the blessings from God.

Day 5
Persistent prayer (Luke 18:1-14)

The purpose of today's lesson: We must persist in prayer.

What is the proper response if we don't get what we pray for?

Show how God desires for us to persist in prayer.

II. Week 2 Ongoing Teaching (Mt 19-21:17, Mk 10-11:19, Lk 18:15-19, Jn 12:1-19)

Day 1
Teachings (Mt 19, Mk 10:1-31, Lk 18:15-30)

The purpose of today's lesson: God will have no idols before Him.

What kept the rich young man out of the Kingdom?

Reveal that God wants us to put our trust in Him alone.

Day 2
Equally paid (Mt 20:1-28, Mk 10:32-45, Lk 18:31-34)

The purpose of today's lesson: God does not want us to concern ourselves with what others receive

Why did some men want to be paid more than others are?

Show that we receive what God wants us to have without concern for what others get.

Day 3
Zaccheus (Mt 20:29-34, Mk 10:46-52, Lk 18:35-19:27)

The purpose of today's lesson: See that Jesus pursued the lost.

Why did Jesus pick Zaccheus out?

Explain that Jesus always gave Himself to the most destitute.

Day 4
Anointing (Jn 12:1-11, Mk 14:3-9, Mt 26:6-13)

The purpose of today's lesson: Nothing given to Jesus is wasted.

Why was Judas upset at Mary?

Discuss that Judas was upset because he was a thief and because he didn't understand who Jesus was.

Day 5
Triumphal entry (Mt 21:1-17, Mk 11:1-19, Lk 19:28-48, Jn 12:12-19)

The purpose of today's lesson: See that the praise of people does not last.

What happened to Jesus one week after this parade?

Explain that Jesus went from celebration to the cross.

III. Week 3 Battle with Religious Leaders (Mt 21:18-23:36; Mk 11:20-12:37; Lk 20:1-44)

The purpose of this week's lesson: See the conflict between true Christianity and religion.

1. Tell how the religious leaders challenged Jesus' authority.

2. Discuss the parable Jesus told at this time

3. Explain how the religious leaders questioned Jesus and His answer to them.

4. Demonstrate Jesus' warning against religious leaders.

IV. Week 4 Preparation for His Death (Mt 23:37-25:46; Mk 13; Lk 21:1-38)

The purpose of this week's lesson: God prepares us for difficult times.

1. Describe Jesus' heart for Jerusalem.

2. Explain Jesus' view of the future and His return.

3. Discuss the importance of being vigilant (watchful).

4. Clarify the story of the ten maidens.

5. Talk about what final judgement will be like.

V. Week 5 Teaching Prior to His Death (Mt 26:1-30; Mk 14:1-26; Lk 22:1-38; Jn 13:1-17:26)

The purpose of this week's lesson: Go over the important teaching Jesus gave before His death.

1. Describe the plot to kill Jesus and Judas' betrayal.

2. Go over in detail Jesus washing the disciples' feet.

3. Explain Jesus' teaching on the Holy Spirit.

4. Elucidate the Last Supper and its purpose.

5. Discuss the prayer of Jesus.

6. Talk about the story of the vine and the branches.

VI. Week 6 Arrest and Trial (Mt 26:31-27:14; Mk 14:27-15:5; Lk 22:39-23:12; Jn 18:1-37)

The purpose of this week's lesson: Understand the unjust nature of the condemnation of Jesus.

1. Discuss the agony of Jesus in the garden.

2. Describe the questioning before the high priests.

3. Explain both visits before Pilate.

4. Elucidate the betrayal and suicide of Judas.

5. Talk about why Jesus ultimately was handed over to be crucified.

VII. Week 7 Crucifixion (Mt 27:15-66; Mk 15:6-47; Lk 23:13-56; Jn 18:38-19:42)

The purpose of this week's lesson: Understand the agony of Jesus' death and how much God loves us.

1. Show how Jesus was mocked before His death.

2. Describe how Jesus carried His cross through the streets.

3. Discuss the crucifixion and Jesus' death.

4. Go over the tomb and the guard placed at the tomb.

VIII. Week 8 Resurrection (Mt 28; Mk 16; Lk 24; Jn 20)

The purpose of this week's lesson: Realize that the grave was not the end of Jesus' life.

1. Describe Jesus' appearance before Mary and the women.

2. Discuss Jesus' walk with the travelers.

3. Explain the story of Jesus feeding the disciples with fish and His talk with Peter.

4. Go over the great commission.

5. Talk about Jesus' ascension.

The Book of Acts

I.   Week 1 Before Pentecost (Acts 1)

Day 1
The Book's Purpose (Acts 1:1, 2)

The purpose of today's lesson: Learn the purpose of the book

What is the purpose for this book?

Discuss the purpose of the book of Acts.

Day 2
Jesus' Life after the Resurrection (Acts 1:3-8)

The purpose of today's lesson: Study what Jesus did after He rose.

What did Jesus do after the resurrection?

Talk about what Jesus did after the resurrection.

Day 3
The Ascension Acts (1:9-11)

The purpose of today's lesson: Look at the Ascension

What did the men say after Jesus ascended?

Consider the conversation after Jesus ascended and it's meaning.

Day 4
Waiting for the Spirit (Acts 1:12-14)

The purpose of today's lesson: See the process of preparing for the coming of the Holy Spirit

What did the church do while waiting for the Spirit?

Discuss this passage emphasizing proper preparation.

Day 5
Choosing a New Apostle (Acts 1:15-26)

The purpose of today's lesson: Understand the choice of leaders

How did the apostles choose a new member?

Explain using this passage how new leaders are chosen.

II.   Week 2 Pentecost (Acts 2, 3)

Day 1
The Spirit Comes (Acts 2:1-13)

The purpose of today's lesson: Study the first time the Spirit came

Why did the men speak in tongues?

Clarify this passage telling how the Spirit came and about speaking in tongues.

Day 2
The First Revival (Acts 2:14-41)

The purpose of today's lesson: Discover the pattern of the first revival

What was Peter's message and the results?

Discuss this passage emphasizing Peter's meaning.

Day 3
Early Fellowship (Acts 2:42-47)

The purpose of today's lesson: Understand how the early church operated

How did the people in the early church spend their time?

Elucidate the way the early fellowship operated.

Day 4
Peter Heals the Lame Man (Acts 3:1-11)

The purpose of today's lesson: Review the first miracle of the church

What did the lame man do after he was healed?

Describe the results of the first miracle.

Day 5
Followup to a Miracle (Acts 3:12-26)

The purpose of today's lesson: See what happens when God moves

What did Peter do after the miracle?

Use this scripture to show how God uses His miracles.

III.   Week 3 Early Persecution (Acts 4-7)

Day 1
Peter Arrested (Acts 4:1-22)

The purpose of today's lesson: Understand the beginning of persecution

What happened to the church after its initial success?

Describe how and why persecution comes.

Day 2
The Spirit's Response (Acts 4:23-37)

The purpose of today's lesson: See God's support during persecution

What does God do when persecution comes?

Explain how God ministers to His people in this time.

Day 3
Death of Traitors (Acts 5:1-16)

The purpose of today's lesson: Know what happens to bad attitudes

Why did Ananias and Sapphira die?

Show that it was their attitude of selfishness that did them in.

Day 4
The Apostles in Prison (Acts 5:17-32)

The purpose of today's lesson: Learn the proper response to persecution

What did Peter mean when he said, "We must obey God rather than men"?

Explain this concept.

Day 5
Gamaliel's Advice (Acts 5:33-42)

The purpose of today's lesson: Discover the response to possible spiritual discovery

What was the basic message of Gamaliel?

Describe how Gamaliel's advice was good advice.

IV.   Week 4 Stephen (Acts 6, 7)

Day 1
Deacons Appointed (Acts 6:1-7)

<u>The purpose of today's lesson</u>: Learn the purpose of deacons

Why were deacons selected?

Discuss the selected of deacons and their job.

Day 2
Witness of Stephen (Acts 6:8-15)

<u>The purpose of today's lesson</u>: See the ministry of a relatively
unimportant person

What sort of man was Stephen?

Show how God used Stephen even though he was a relatively
unimportant part of the church.

Day 3 & 4
Message of Stephen (Acts 7:1-53)

<u>The purpose of today's lesson</u>: Learn the essence of important messages

What did Stephen say when he spoke and why?

Describe the message of Stephen emphasizing that Stephen reviewed
God's work and related that to why people missed God.

Day 5
Stephen Martyred (Acts 7:54-60)

<u>The purpose of today's lesson</u>: Learn even when you do good people don't listen

Why was Stephen martyred?

Show that hard-hearted people are difficult to change.

V. Week 5 The Church Scattered (Acts 8, 9)

Day 1
Philip (Acts 8:1-8)

<u>The purpose of today's lesson</u>: Realize as persecution comes the gospel is spread

Why did Philip go down to Samaria?

Explain that as the church is persecuted it spread.

Day 2
Simon the Sorcerer (Acts 8:9-25)

<u>The purpose of today's lesson</u>: Discover that the gift of God cannot be bought

What was Simon trying to buy?

Discuss this scripture showing what Simon was buying and why he couldn't buy it.

Day 3
Philip and the Ethiopian (Acts 8:26-40)

<u>The purpose of today's lesson</u>: We need to go where God is moving

How did Philip know the Ethiopian was ready for the Gospel?

Explain how when we go where God wants He will use us

Day 4
Conversion of Saul (Acts 9:1-19)

The purpose of today's lesson: See that God knocks us off our high horse

How did God save Saul?

Discuss the conversion of Saul.

Day 5
Continued Ministry (Acts 9:20-43)

The purpose of today's lesson: Miraculous conversions lead to ministry

What did Saul (Paul) do after his conversion?

Talk about the ministry of Paul after his conversion.

VI.   Week 6 Gentiles Join the Church (Acts 10, 11)

Day 1
Visions (Acts 10:1-22)

The purpose of today's lesson: God prepares us for big changes

Why did God give Peter this vision?

Show that God precedes big changes with His Word.

Day 2
Conversion of Cornelius (Acts 10:23-48)

The purpose of today's lesson: God will convert the faithful man.

Why did God speak to Cornelius, a non-Jew.

Discuss that God will speak to faithful men no matter who they are.

Day 3
Peter (Acts 11:1-18)

The purpose of today's lesson: God will give you evidence for your ministry

How did God confirm Peter's work?

Explain that when you are doing God's work God will confirm it.

Day 4
Antioch (Acts 11:19-30)

The purpose of today's lesson: When a new church is established the recognized churches support it.

Why did Jerusalem believers go to Antioch?

Discuss how the established churches support new church plants.

VII. Week 7 Further Persecution and Deliverance (Acts 12)

Day 1
Death of James (Acts 12:1-4)

The purpose of today's lesson: While the church grows persecution continues

Why was James killed?

Discussed that James was killed but Peter was preserved.

Day 2
Peter Delivered (Acts 12:5-12)

The purpose of today's lesson: No matter how bad things get God preserves His church

How was Peter delivered?

Teach that God will always preserve His work despite the opposition.

Day 3
Rhoda (Acts 12:13-19)

The purpose of today's lesson: We are frequently unprepared for God's deliverance

Why did Rhoda rum off leaving Peter at the door?

Explain how we are often unprepared for God's work.

Day 4
Herod Dies (Acts 12:20-25)

The purpose of today's lesson: People are struck down in their pride

What happened to Herod and why?

Show that God does not put up with arrogance forever.

VIII. Week 8 Paul's First Missionary Journey (Acts 13, 14)

Day 1
Paul and Barnabas (Acts 13:1-13)

The purpose of today's lesson: God separates out the people He wants

How were Paul and Barnabas chosen?

Use this passage to show that God separates the people He wants.

Day 2
Antioch (Acts 13:14-52)

The purpose of today's lesson: The speaker changes but the message is the same

What did Paul preach about?

Show that Paul preached the same thing that Peter did.

Day 3
The Galatian Country

The purpose of today's lesson: Review what the people were like that Paul ministered to.

What were these people like?

If you still have, What the Bible is all about, by Mears, look up Galacia and talk about this area. If not use other reference books.

Day 4
Iconium (Acts 14:1-7)

The purpose of today's lesson: The gospel has caused and will cause great conflict in the world

Why were the people in this city divided?

Discuss how when the gospel was preached the Jews responded by stirring up division.

Day 5
Lystra (Acts 14:8-28)

The purpose of today's lesson: God gives signs and wonders to establish credibility

What was the purpose of the healing by Paul in Lystra?

Explain that God gives signs and wonders to establish minister's credibility.

IX.   Week 9 Counsel at Jerusalem (Acts 15)

Day 1
Question of Circumcision (Acts 15:1-6)

The purpose of today's lesson: Old traditions die hard but must die if contrary to the gospel

What was the source of the argument at the counsel?

Describe how Jewish Christians wanted to require circumcision of gentiles.

Day 2
Case Presented (Acts 15:7-13)

The purpose of today's lesson: God gives evidence for changes in His ways

What was Peter's main reason for not requiring circumcision?

Show that God moved through the gentiles without requiring circumcision.

Day 3
Paul supports Peter (Acts 15:14-21)

The purpose of today's lesson: God will use more than 1 witness

Why did Paul support Peter?

Describe how Paul's ministry supported Peter's argument and how God uses more than one witness in important matters.

Day 4
Decision of the Counsel Announced (Acts 15:22-35)

The purpose of today's lesson: Men who hear God announce God's decision.

Whose opinion was reflected in the decision?

Discuss the decision of the counsel emphasizing that this was God's decision and not men's.

Day 5
Plans for the Second Trip (Acts 15:36-42)

The purpose of today's lesson: Even Godly men disagree

What was the source of the fight between Paul and Barnabas?

Read this passage showing that Godly men have disagreements.

X.   Week 10 Paul's Second Missionary Journey (Acts 16-18)

Day 1
Galatians (Acts 16:1-5)

The purpose of today's lesson: Sometimes it is good to comply with tradition rather than fight

Why did Paul circumcise Timothy?

Show that Paul did this to keep the focus on the gospel and not on side issues.

Day 2
Philippians (Acts 16:6-40)

The purpose of today's lesson: Men of God are sensitive to the Spirit.

How did Paul end up in Philippi?

Discuss how Paul was going one way but the Spirit sent him elsewhere.

Day 3
Thessalonica and Berea (Acts 17:1-14)

The purpose of today's lesson: Some people are more open to truth

What made the Bereans better than the Thessalonians?

Explain how the Bereans were nobler.

Day 4
Athens (Acts 17:15-34)

The purpose of today's lesson: Every man desires God

What was the theme of Paul's message on the Areopagus?

Show that Paul recognized that all men desire God and just need to know who God is.

Day 5
Corinth (Acts 18)

The purpose of today's lesson: The man of God needs encouragement from time to time

Why did God appear to Paul in the vision in Corinth?

Describe Paul's ministry in Corinth especially how God appeared to him to encourage him.

XI. Week 11 Paul's Third Missionary Journey (Acts 19, 20)

Day 1
Ephesus, the Spirit Comes (Acts 19:1-7)

The purpose of today's lesson: John's baptism was not enough

What did Paul do when he came to Ephesus?

Describe how Paul ministered to the Ephesians.

Day 2
Ephesus, in the Temple (Acts 19:8-41)

The purpose of today's lesson: Before confronting evil make sure you know God

What happened with the seven sons of Sceva?
Show that one cannot use someone else's faith in ministry.

Day 3
Macedonia (Acts 20:1-4)

The purpose of today's lesson: When you are successful men may plot your downfall

What did the Jews do when he came to Macedonia?

Explain the point here is the plot against Paul's life.

Day 4
Troas (Acts 20:5-12)

The purpose of today's lesson: God does not forsake the faithful

What happened to the boy who fell to sleep during Paul's message?

Tell the story of this boy who was raised from the dead.

Day 5
Miletus (Acts 20:13-38)

The purpose of today's lesson: Continue in God even when facing trials

Did Paul know he faced persecution?

Explain how Paul knew trials were coming but continued in God.

XII. Week 12 Paul is Arrested (Acts 21, 22)

Day 1
Tyre (Acts 21:1-7)

The purpose of today's lesson: People around Paul tried to stop him

What advice did Paul receive from his friends?

Discuss how well meaning people will try to protect the man of God.

Day 2
Caesarea (Acts 21:8-14)

The purpose of today's lesson: Despite well-meaning friends Paul would not be stopped

What was Paul's response to his well-meaning friends?

Show that Paul was undeterred by his friends.

Day 3
Jerusalem (Acts 21:15-40)

The purpose of today's lesson: In Jerusalem Paul did not have a chance

Why was Paul arrested?

Clarify that the Romans arrested Paul to protect him.

Day 4
The Mob (Acts 22:1-24)

The purpose of today's lesson: When faced with a mob. Paul gives his testimony

What is the theme of Paul's message to the mob?

Discuss that a testimony is a very powerful approach.

Day 5
Citizenship (Acts 22:25-30)

The purpose of today's lesson: Paul did everything he could to keep his message alive

Why did Paul invoke his citizenship?

Demonstrate that Paul refuse to fade away quietly.

XIII. Week 13 Paul's Defense (Acts 23-26)

Day 1
Defense in Jerusalem (Acts 23:1-22)

The purpose of today's lesson: Paul was given little chance by the Jews to defend himself

How much was Paul able to say in Jerusalem?

The point here is the Jews were not interested in fairness

Day 2
Caesarea (Acts 23:23-35)

The purpose of today's lesson: Paul goes from the frying pan into the fire

How was Paul's arrest like that of Jesus?

Explain that Paul was arrested by the Romans to protect him from the Jews over issues of the Law.

Day 3
Felix (Acts 24)

The purpose of today's lesson: Learn man's favorite excuse

What is man's favorite excuse?

Show that Felix, not knowing what to do, didn't do anything (There is no hurry).

Day 4
Festus (Acts 25)

The purpose of today's lesson: Discipline will cultivate maturity

What was Paul's message to Festus?

Despite years in prison and continuing false accusation Paul stayed true to his message.

Day 5
Agrippa (Acts 26)

The purpose of today's lesson: Learn the importance of the word "almost".

What was important about the fact Agrippa "almost" became a Christian?

Discuss how "almost" can be so frustrating in life.

XIV. Week 14 Paul's Trip to Rome (Acts 27, 28)

Day 1
Journey to Rome (Acts 27:1-13)

The purpose of today's lesson: One should listen to the warnings of God's man

What was Paul's warning?

Discuss the trip and the warning that went unheeded.

Day 2
Ship Wreck (Acts 27:14-44)

The purpose of today's lesson: A disaster is not always so bad

Why was this shipwreck not so bad?

Explain how this accident was a good thing.

Day 3
Melita (Acts 28:1-10)

The purpose of today's lesson: When God has a plan nothing can stop it

Why didn't Paul die after the snakebite?

Show that God wanted Paul to make it to Rome.

Day 4
More Travel (Acts 28:11-15)

The purpose of today's lesson: Paul reached his goal despite astounding opposition

What did Paul go through to reach Rome?

Recount all that Paul had to do to reach his goal, Rome.

Day 5
Paul in Rome (Acts 28:16-31)

The purpose of today's lesson: Once in Rome Paul spent all his time preaching the gospel

When you reach your goal, what should you do?

Describe how Paul spent all his time preaching once he reached Rome.

FOUNDATIONS OF THE CHRISTIAN LIFE

I.   Week 1 Salvation

Day 1 Acts 2:14-40
What must I do to be saved?

The purpose of today's lesson: Starting talking about salvation and the importance of salvation.

When Peter spoke to all those people, what was the main message?

Tell the story of Acts 2 emphasizing the message of salvation. Mom or dad should share their testimony.

Day 2 Romans 5
Saved by faith

The purpose of today's lesson: Show that faith is necessary for salvation.

What is necessary in us for us to be saved?

Discuss Romans 5 emphasizing that our faith is necessary for us to be saved. Mom or Dad should share their testimony.

Day 3 Acts 4:1-31
Salvation in no other

The purpose of today's lesson: Learn that Jesus is the only source of salvation.

Why are people who believe in Mohammed or Buddha not saved?

Tell the story of Acts 4. Make sure your child understands that earnest faith is not enough but faith must be in Jesus.

Day 4 Matthew 28:19-20; Romans 1:16; I Cor 9:22
Salvation is for everyone

The purpose of today's lesson: Understand that salvation is for all people.

Is there anyone who cannot be saved?

Go over the scriptures showing that salvation is for all and we are called to minister to all.

Day 5 Luke 16:20-31
Salvation from eternal judgement

<u>The purpose of today's lesson</u>: **Study what we are ultimately saved from.**

What happens to people whom are not saved?

Tell the story of Lazarus showing that people who are not saved face eternal punishment.

II. Week 2 Repentance

Day 1 Gen. 6:5,7; Jer 4:28
What is repentance?

<u>The purpose of today's lesson</u>: **Understand what repentance is.**

What dose the word repent mean?

Go over the scriptures making sure the children understand that repent means to turn away from one thing and toward another.

Day 2 Acts 3:12-19; Act 2:37-41
The necessity of repentance

<u>The purpose of today's lesson</u>: **See that repentance is the first step to God.**

What was Peter's first instruction to people who wanted to turn to God?

Tell these two stories showing that repent was Peter's first instruction.

Day 3 Heb 6:1; Heb 9:14
Repent from dead works

<u>The purpose of today's lesson</u>: **Learn what we repent from.**

What are dead works?

Discuss these scriptures showing what dead works are giving examples from your own life.

Day 4 II Sam 11:1-12:23; Psalm 51
An example of repentance

<u>The purpose of today's lesson</u>: **See the life of someone who repented.**

Was David sorry over what he did?

Tell this story emphasizing David's heart once his sin was exposed.

Day 5 Luke 13:1-8
Results of an unrepentant heart

<u>The purpose of today's lesson</u>: **Understand the results of refusing to repent.**

What happens to people who do not repent?

This is a difficult story. Judgement is in store for all who do not repent.

III. Week 3 Faith

Day 1 Hebrews 11:1
What is faith?

<u>The purpose of today's lesson</u>: **Learn what faith is**

What is faith?

Use this scripture to start defining faith.

Day 2 Hebrews 11:6; Habbakkuk 2:4
The necessity of faith

<u>The purpose of today's lesson</u>: **Understand that faith is essential**

Give two reasons faith is so important.

Use this scripture to explain why faith is important.

Day 3 Hebrews 11
Men of faith

The purpose of today's lesson: To see faith in action

Who is your favorite man of faith?

Tell the story of some of these men of faith and give your own testimony of faith.

Day 4 I John 5:10-13; John 8:30-36
Have faith in Jesus

The purpose of today's lesson: See that our faith needs to be in Jesus

Why do we have faith in Jesus?

Discuss the scriptures emphasizing the need to have faith in Jesus.

Day 5 John 3:36; John 5:24
Faith in Jesus alone

The purpose of today's lesson: See that it is not just faith but faith in Jesus

What happens to people who believe in Mohammed?

Discuss the scripture making the point that faith is only as good as its object.

IV. Week 4 Baptisms

Day 1 Romans 6:3-6
Baptized into His death

The purpose of today's lesson: See the real meaning of baptism in water.

When a person goes under water, what is happening to them?

Explain the theology of baptism in water as joining Christ in His burial and resurrection.

Day 2 Col 2:12, John 3:5
Buried with Him

The purpose of today's lesson: Reiterate the meaning of water baptism.

What does it mean to be buried with Christ?

Mom and Dad give your testimony about when you were baptized.

> Day 3 Matt 28:19-20
> Baptized in Jesus' name

<u>**The purpose of today's lesson**</u>: **Understand the meaning of baptism in Jesus' name.**

What does it mean to be baptized in Jesus' name?

Explain baptism in Jesus' name.

> Day 4 Acts 2:1-4
> Rushing wind

<u>**The purpose of today's lesson**</u>: **Gain a beginning understanding of baptism in the Holy Spirit.**

What is the baptism in the Holy Spirit?

Mom and Dad, give your testimony in this area.

> Day 5 Acts 1:8; Acts 4:13-14; 4:24-33
> Receiving power

<u>**The purpose of today's lesson**</u>: **Realize the main reason for the baptism in the Holy Spirit.**

What is the primary ministry when the Holy Ghost comes?

Explain that power to speak boldly for God is the main ministry of the Holy Spirit.

V.   Week 5 Worship

> Day 1 Gen 22:1-14
> First worship

<u>**The purpose of today's lesson**</u>: Introduce worship

What was Abraham's form of worship?

Tell this story emphasizes that the sacrifice was Abraham's worship and Isaac was a type of Christ.

Day 2 Ex 34:14-17
No other gods

The purpose of today's lesson: Understand that God allows worship of no other.

What does God think of the worship of other gods?

Explain that God allows the worship of no other gods.

Day 3 Ps 22:22-31
In the congregation

The purpose of today's lesson: Learn that worship is appropriate in a gathering of believers.

Is worship appropriate with others?

Explain that worship in the congregation is one thing God has called us to.

Day 4 Ps 22:3
God inhabits praise

The purpose of today's lesson: Understand the ministry of praise.

What happens when God's people praise Him?

Give most important result of praise

Day 5 I Sam 15:24-31
Sin prevents our worship

The purpose of today's lesson: See the main reason we cannot praise.

What prevents us from praising God?

Explain how sin effects our praise and why using the story of Saul.

VI. Week 6 The Church

Day 1 Matt 16:13-19
Foundation of the church

The purpose of today's lesson: Learn the foundation of the church.

What is the foundation of the church?

Use these scriptures to show Christ as the foundation of the church

    Day 2 Acts 2:47
    Sanctuary for believers

The purpose of today's lesson: Learn one function of the church.

What is one function of the church?

Explain the church as a place for believers. Make sure the children know that the church is the believers not a building.

    Day 3 Acts 15
    Dealing with difficulties

The purpose of today's lesson: Learn a second function of the church.

What is another important ministry of the church?

Use the story to explain the church as a place where disputes are resolved.

    Day 4 I Cor 14
    Spiritual gifts to the church

The purpose of today's lesson: Know the operation of spiritual gifts in the church.

How do the gifts work in the church?

Use this chapter to discuss spiritual gifts in the church and their purpose.

    Day 5 Heb 10:24-25
    Necessity of fellowship

The purpose of today's lesson: Discuss the need for fellowship.

Why do we need fellowship?

Explain the need for relationship (encouragement and accountability).

Made in the USA
Middletown, DE
15 September 2019